Collins

Collins Foundation World Atlas

D1439351

Collins
An imprint of HarperCollinsPublishers
77-85 Fulham Palace Road
LondonW6 8JB

© HarperCollinsPublishers 2005
Maps © Bartholomew Ltd 2005

First published 2005
ISBN 0 00 719547 8 (Educational edition)
ISBN 0 00 719546 X (Trade edition)

RL 11784 Imp 001

Collins ® is a registered trademark of
HarperCollinsPublishers Ltd

The contents of this edition of the Collins
Foundation World Atlas are believed correct at the
time of printing. Nevertheless the publishers can
accept no responsibility for errors or omissions,
changes in the detail given, or for any expense or
loss thereby caused.

Printed and bound in Thailand

British Library Cataloguing in Publication Data
A catalogue record for this book is available from
the British Library.

All mapping in this atlas is generated from Collins
Bartholomew digital databases. Collins
Bartholomew, the UK's leading independent
geographical information supplier, can provide a
digital, custom, and premium mapping service to a
variety of markets. For further information:
Tel: +44 (0) 141 306 3752
e-mail: collinsbartholomew@harpercollins.co.uk

Visit our website at: www.collinsbartholomew.com

everything clicks at www.collins.co.uk

A Political Map

Map A uses different colours to show clearly the shape of each country. A line is used to represent the international boundary around each country. It is possible to see the relative areas of the countries. Capital cities and other major cities are shown by symbols on a Political map.

B Rainfall Map

The colours on Map B represent areas which have the same range of annual rainfall. From this type of map it is possible to find the wettest or driest region in a country. Rainfall maps are often accompanied by climate graphs such as the one shown at the bottom of the opposite page.

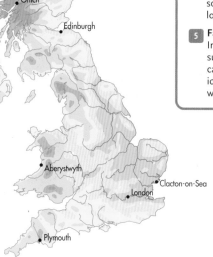

Using Atlas Maps

An atlas includes different kinds of maps and diagram. The different parts of an atlas page are shown on the map below which is a reduced version of page 22 in the atlas. In order to understand maps it is important to understand the labels and information which appear on each page. The example below is a reference map whi

Using Atlas Maps

1 Page Title
The page title explains what area or topic the map covers.

2 Page Number
The page number is essential when using the index or contents page.

3 Letters and Numbers
These form a grid which make it easy to find places listed in the index eg Naples is in grid square F4.

4 Lines of Latitude
These show how far north or south of the Equator a place is located.

5 Facts Box
Information in the Facts Box is subdivided into various categories. An icon (or symbol) identifies each of the categories which are explained below.

Facts Box...
The information listed in the **Facts about...** box is explained below.

Landscape: Indicates the area and highest point.

Population: Lists the total population and the average number of people living in one square kilometre.

Settlement: Shows the percentage of the population living in cities and towns. The main towns and cities are also listed.

Land Use: Main crops grown and the main industries in the region are identified here.

Development Indicators: Four indicators are shown here.

Life expectancy: The number of years a newborn child can expect to survive.
GNP per capita: The annual value of production of goods and services of a country, per person.
Primary school enrolment: The total of all ages enrolled at primary level as a percentage of primary age children.
Access to safe water: Percentage of the population with reasonable access to sufficient safe water.

...ows a variety of information such as settlement, ...mmunications, the physical landscape and political ...orders. In this atlas there are also many thematic ...aps which give information on one or two special ...pics. Maps A, B, C and D to the left and right of the ...ference map are typical examples of four different ...pes of thematic map.

C Relief Map

Map C shows the height of the land. Areas which are the same height above sea level are shown in the same colour. Lowland is shown in green and the highest mountain areas in brown or purple. The landscape features are named on a relief map and symbols are used to show the main mountain peaks. From this map we can see that Kilimanjaro is the highest peak in Africa.

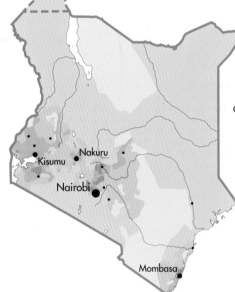

Using Atlas Maps

6 Locator Map
The locator map shows the position of the map in a wider region.

7 Key Box
Every map has a key which explains the symbols used on the map. The use of symbols on the maps in this atlas are explained in more detail on page 6.

8 Scale Bar and Ratio Scale

9 Lines of Longitude
These show how far east or west of the Greenwich Meridian a place is located.

10 Compass
The compass shows the direction of north, south, east and west. Maps are usually drawn with north at the top of the page.

11 Projection Note

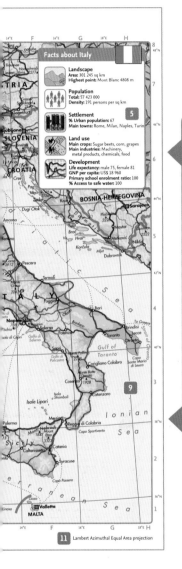

Facts about Italy

Landscape
Area: 301 245 sq km
Highest point: Mont Blanc 4808 m

Population
Total: 57 423 000
Density: 191 persons per sq km

Settlement
% Urban population: 67
Main towns: Rome, Milan, Naples, Turin

Land use
Main crops: Sugar beets, corn, grapes
Main industries: Machinery, metal products, chemicals, food

Development
Life expectancy: male 75, female 81
GNP per capita: US$ 18 960
Primary school enrolment ratio: 100
% Access to safe water: 100

11 Lambert Azimuthal Equal Area projection

D Population Map

The colours used on this map show the distribution of the population in the rural areas. Different sizes of dot show the distribution of cities and towns. Together the different colours and different size dots show where most of the people of Kenya live.

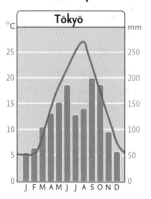

Graphs

...information in this atlas is often ...resented as a graph or diagram. ...hree examples of graphs used ...re shown to the right.
...ie graphs are circles divided into ...egments to show percentage ...alues.
...ar graphs can be used to ...ompare production values of ...everal topics.
...limate graphs are a combination ...f bars and lines.

Pie Graph

- Forest
- Arable
- Pasture
- Other

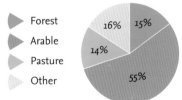

15%
16%
14%
55%

Bar Graph

Agriculture, Forestry, Fisheries
Construction
Manufacturing
Services

0 10 20 30 40 50 60 70

Primary   Secondary   Tertiary

Percentage employed by economic sector

Climate Graph

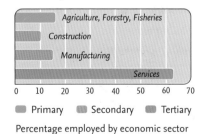

Tōkyō

Latitude and Longitude

Lines of latitude are imaginary lines which run in an east-west direction around the globe. They run parallel to each other and are measured in degrees, written as °. The most important line of latitude is the **Equator**, 0°. All other lines of latitude have a value between 0° and 90° North or South of the Equator. 90° north is the North Pole and, 90° south, the South Pole.

Lines of longitude are imaginary lines which run in a north-south direction between the **North Pole** and the **South Pole.** The most important line of longitude is 0°, the **Greenwich Meridian**, which runs through the Greenwich Observatory in London. Exactly opposite the Greenwich Meridian on the other side of the world, is the 180° line of longitude. All other lines of longitude are measured in degrees east or west of 0°.

When both lines of latitude and longitude are drawn on a map they form a grid. It is easy to find a place on the map if the latitude and longitude values are known. The point of intersection of the line of latitude and the line of longitude locates the place exactly.

The Equator can be used to divide the globe into two halves. Land north of the Equator is the **Northern Hemisphere.** Land south of the Equator is the **Southern Hemisphere.** The 0° and 180° lines of longitude can also be used to divide the globe into two halves, the **Western** and **Eastern Hemispheres.** Together, the Equator and 0° and 180°, divide the world into four areas, for example, North America is in the Northern Hemisphere and the Western Hemisphere.

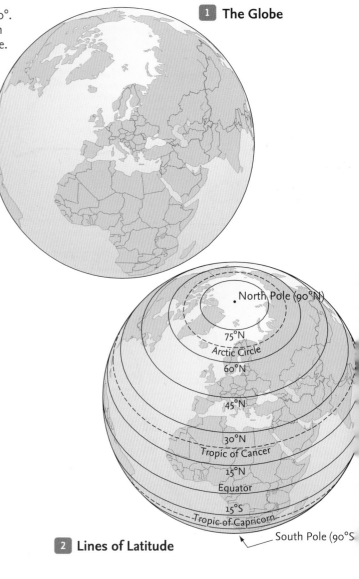

1 The Globe

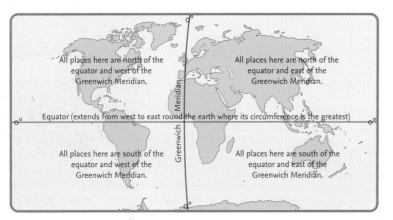

All places here are north of the equator and west of the Greenwich Meridian.

All places here are north of the equator and east of the Greenwich Meridian.

Equator (extends from west to east round the earth where its circumference is the greatest)

All places here are south of the equator and west of the Greenwich Meridian.

All places here are south of the equator and east of the Greenwich Meridian.

Greenwich Meridian

North Pole (90°N)

75°N

Arctic Circle

60°N

45°N

30°N

Tropic of Cancer

15°N

Equator

15°S

Tropic of Capricorn

South Pole (90°S)

2 Lines of Latitude

Using Scale

The **scale** of each map in this atlas is shown in two ways:

1 The **Ratio scale** is written, for example, as 1 : 1 000 000.
This means that one unit of measurement on the map represents 1 000 000 of the same unit on the ground.

eg **Scale 1 : 1 000 000**

2 The **line** or **bar scale** shows the scale as a line with the distance on the ground marked at intervals along the line.

Different Scales

The three maps to the right cover the same area of the page but are at different scales. Map A is a large scale map which shows a small area in detail. Map C is a small scale map which means it shows a larger area in the same space as Map A, however in much less detail. The area of Map A is highlighted on maps B and C. As the scale ratio increases the map becomes smaller.

Scale 1 : 3 000 000

Map A

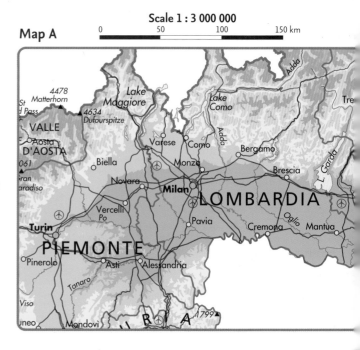

Lines of Latitude and Longitude [4]

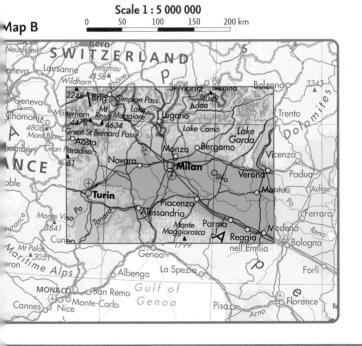

Measuring Distance

The scale of a map can also be used to work out how far it is between two places. In the example below, the straight line distance between Brasília and Salvador on the map of Brazil is 7 cm. The scale of the map is 1 : 15 000 000. Therefore 7 cm on the map represents 7 X 15 000 000 cm or 105 000 000 cm on the ground. Converted to kilometres this is 1050 km. The real distance between Brasília and Salvador is therefore 1050 km on the ground.

Scale 1 : 15 000 000

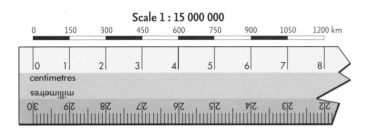

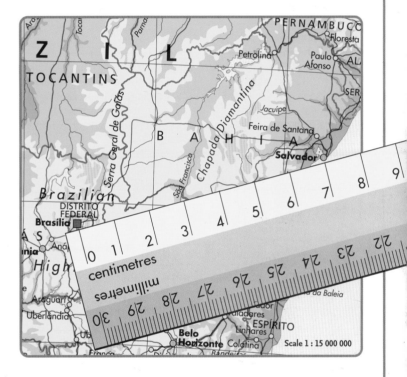

[3] Lines of Longitude

Map B

Scale 1 : 5 000 000

Map C

Scale 1 : 15 000 000

Symbols

Maps use **symbols** to show the location of a feature and to give information about that feature. The symbols used on each map in this atlas are explained in the **key** to each map.

Symbols used on maps can be dots, diagrams, lines or area colours. They vary in colour, size and shape. The numbered captions to the map below help explain some of the symbols used on the maps in this atlas.

Different styles of type are also used to show differences between features, for example, country names are shown in large bold capitals, small water features, rivers and lakes in small italics.

Using Grids

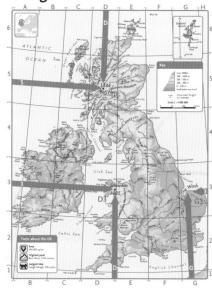

The map on the left shows the British Isles. Lines of latitude and longitude are numbered in 2° intervals in the map frame. These form a **grid** on the map. Large letters and numbers, together known as **alphanumerics,** are used to label the horizontal and vertical columns made by the grid.

The alphanumerics can be used to identify the **grid square** in which a feature is located, for example

Ben Nevis is in D5,
Snowdon in D3,
The Wash in G3.

1	~	**River** The largest and most important rivers are shown.
2	✈	**Airport** Main international airports are shown.
3	◉	**Large City** This symbol is used to show cities with over 500 000 people.
4	■	**Capital City** All capital cities, large or small are shown with the same symbol.
5	╱	**Railway** **Road** Railways and roads are the main links between the towns and cities.
6	◠	**Lake** Lakes and areas of water are shown in a pale blue tint.
7	○	**Other Town or City** Cities or towns with less than 500 000 people are shown as a small yellow dot.
8	╲	**International Boundary** International boundaries mark the edges between one country and another. They give a country a distinctive shape by which we can often identify it.

A. ANDORRA
L. LIECHTENSTEIN
LUX. LUXEMBOURG
M. MONACO
ETH. NETHERLANDS
S.M. SAN MARINO

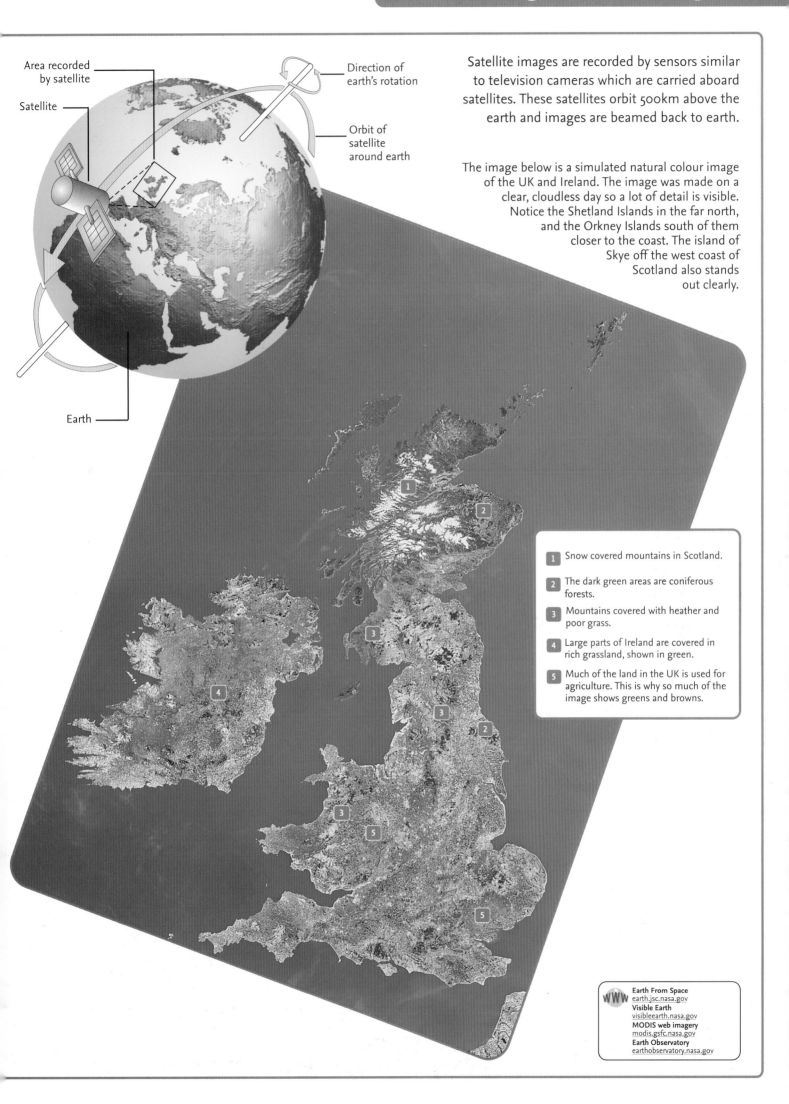

Area recorded by satellite

Satellite

Earth

Direction of earth's rotation

Orbit of satellite around earth

Satellite images are recorded by sensors similar to television cameras which are carried aboard satellites. These satellites orbit 500km above the earth and images are beamed back to earth.

The image below is a simulated natural colour image of the UK and Ireland. The image was made on a clear, cloudless day so a lot of detail is visible. Notice the Shetland Islands in the far north, and the Orkney Islands south of them closer to the coast. The island of Skye off the west coast of Scotland also stands out clearly.

1 Snow covered mountains in Scotland.

2 The dark green areas are coniferous forests.

3 Mountains covered with heather and poor grass.

4 Large parts of Ireland are covered in rich grassland, shown in green.

5 Much of the land in the UK is used for agriculture. This is why so much of the image shows greens and browns.

WWW **Earth From Space**
earth.jsc.nasa.gov
Visible Earth
visibleearth.nasa.gov
MODIS web imagery
modis.gsfc.nasa.gov
Earth Observatory
earthobservatory.nasa.gov

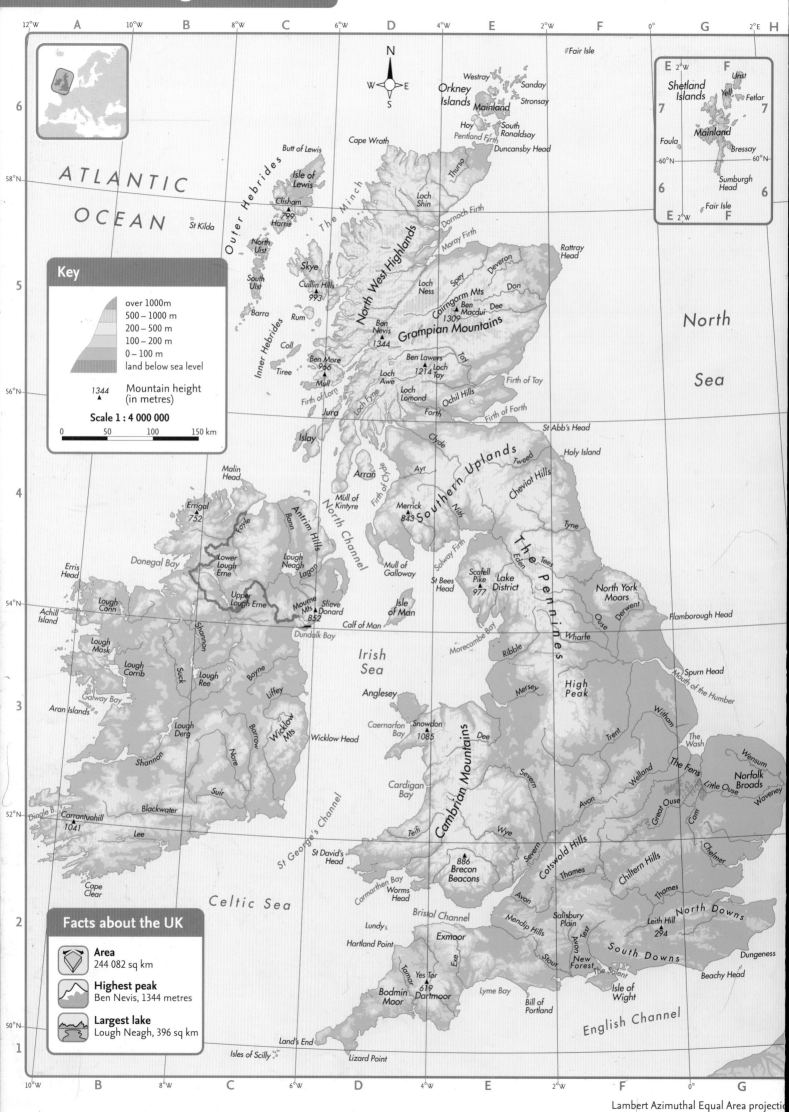

Key

- over 1000m
- 500 – 1000 m
- 200 – 500 m
- 100 – 200 m
- 0 – 100 m
- land below sea level

▲ 1344 Mountain height (in metres)

Scale 1 : 4 000 000

0   50   100   150 km

Facts about the UK

Area
244 082 sq km

Highest peak
Ben Nevis, 1344 metres

Largest lake
Lough Neagh, 396 sq km

ATLANTIC OCEAN

North Sea

Irish Sea

Celtic Sea

English Channel

Shetland Islands
Mainland
Foula
Unst
Yell
Fetlar
Bressay
Sumburgh Head
Fair Isle

Fair Isle
Westray
Sanday
Orkney Islands
Mainland
Stronsay
Hoy
Pentland Firth
South Ronaldsay
Duncansby Head
Cape Wrath
Thurso

Butt of Lewis
Outer Hebrides
Isle of Lewis
Clisham 799
Harris
North Uist
South Uist
Barra
St Kilda
The Minch
Loch Shin
Dornoch Firth
Moray Firth
Rattray Head
Deveron
Spey
Don
Dee
Cairngorm Mts
Ben Macdui 1309
North West Highlands
Skye
Cuillin Hills 993
Rum
Coll
Tiree
Mull
Firth of Lorn
Jura
Islay
Ben Nevis 1344
Loch Ness
Loch Awe
Loch Tyne
Ben More 966
Grampian Mountains
Ben Lawers 1214
Loch Tay
Tay
Firth of Tay
Loch Lomond
Ochil Hills
Forth
Firth of Forth
Inner Hebrides

Malin Head
Errigal 752
Foyle
Bann
Antrim Hills
Donegal Bay
Lower Lough Erne
Lough Neagh
Lagan
Upper Lough Erne
Mourne Mts
Slieve Donard 852
Dundalk Bay
North Channel
Mull of Kintyre
Firth of Clyde
Arran
Ayr
Merrick 843
Southern Uplands
Nith
Solway Firth
Mull of Galloway
St Bees Head
Isle of Man
Calf of Man
Clyde
Tweed
St Abb's Head
Holy Island
Cheviot Hills
Tyne
Eden
Tees
The Pennines
Scafell Pike 977
Lake District
Derwent
North York Moors
Flamborough Head
Wharfe
Ouse
Morecambe Bay
Ribble
High Peak
Mersey
Spurn Head
Mouth of the Humber

Erris Head
Lough Conn
Achill Island
Lough Mask
Lough Corrib
Galway Bay
Aran Islands
Lough Ree
Suck
Shannon
Lough Derg
Boyne
Liffey
Barrow
Nore
Suir
Wicklow Mts
Wicklow Head
Anglesey
Caernarfon Bay
Snowdon 1085
Dee
Cambrian Mountains
Cardigan Bay
Teifi
St George's Channel
St David's Head
Carmarthen Bay
Worms Head
886 Brecon Beacons
Wye
Severn
Avon
Severn
Cotswold Hills
Thames
Trent
Witham
The Wash
The Fens
Norfolk Broads
Wensum
Little Ouse
Waveney
Great Ouse
Cam
Welland
Avon
Chelmer
Chiltern Hills
Thames
North Downs
Leith Hill 294
South Downs
Dungeness
Beachy Head

Dingle B.
Carrantuohill 1041
Lee
Blackwater
Cape Clear
Shannon
Bristol Channel
Lundy
Hartland Point
Exmoor
Yes Tor 619
Dartmoor
Bodmin Moor
Tamar
Exe
Lyme Bay
Bill of Portland
Mendip Hills
Salisbury Plain
Avon
Test
Stour
New Forest
The Solent
Isle of Wight
Land's End
Isles of Scilly
Lizard Point

Lambert Azimuthal Equal Area projectio

Key

——	Country boundary
——	Internal boundary
——	Road
——	Railway
··········	Ferry route
✈	Airport
■	Capital city
●	Large town or city
○	Other town or city

Scale 1 : 4 000 000

0   50   100   150 km

National Statistics Online
www.statistics.gov.uk
Department for Transport
www.dft.gov.uk
UK at a glance
www.statistics.gov.uk/glance

Key

	Country boundary
	Regional boundary
	Road
	Railway
✈	Airport
■	Capital city
●	Large town or city
○	Other town or city

1000 – 2000 m
500 – 1000 m
200 – 500 m
100 – 200 m
0 – 100 m
land below sea level

▲ 1344 Mountain height (in metres)

River

Lake

Scale 1 : 3 000 000

0   30   60   90   120 km

N
W E
S

Shetland Islands
Unst
Yell
Mainland
Bressay
Lerwick
Sumburgh Head

Fair Isle

North Ronaldsay
Westray
Orkney Islands
Mainland Kirkwall
Hoy
South Ronaldsay
John o'Groats
Wick

Thurso
Helmsdale
Dornoch Firth
Moray Firth

Cape Wrath
Durness
Loch Shin
Ben Wyvis
1046
Dingwall
Inverness
Loch Ness
Fort Augustus

Ullapool
An Teallach
1062
North West Highlands

Butt of Lewis
Stornoway
Clisham
799
Harris
Isle of Lewis

Outer Hebrides

Lochmaddy
North Uist
South Uist
Lochboisdale
Barra

St Kilda

The Minch

Uig
Portree
Skye
Kyle of Lochalsh
Mallaig
Fort William
Ben Nevis
1344

Rum
Eigg
Tobermory
Mull
Coll
Tiree
Inner Hebrides
Firth of Lorn
Oban

SCOTLAND
Elgin
Aviemore
Ben Macdui
1309
Grampian Mountains
Blair Atholl
Pitlochry

Banff
Huntly
Deveron
Don
Dee
Aberdeen
Stonehaven
Fraserburgh
Rattray Head
Peterhead

Montrose
Arbroath
Forfar
N. Esk
S. Esk
Tay
Loch Tay
Perth
Dundee
St Andrews
Firth of Tay
Glenrothes
Kirkcaldy
Dunfermline
Firth of Forth

Loch Lomond
Crianlarich
Ben More
1174
Stirling
Falkirk
Livingston
Ochil Hills
Dunbar
Edinburgh

Inveraray
Lochgilphead
Greenock
Dumbarton
Clydebank
Paisley
Glasgow
Motherwell
Hamilton
East Kilbride
Rothesay
Jura
Arran
Firth of Clyde
Irvine
Kilmarnock
Prestwick
Ayr

Port Askaig
Islay
Port Ellen
Campbeltown

Berwick-upon-Tweed
Coldstream
Galashiels
Jedburgh
Hawick
Peebles
Moffat
Southern Uplands
Alnwick

Malin Head

North Sea

ATLANTIC OCEAN

10°W   8°W   6°W   4°W   2°W   0°   2°E

60°N
58°N
56°N

Facts about United Kingdom

Landscape
Area: 244 082 sq km
Highest point: Ben Nevis 1344 m

Population
Total: 59 756 000
Density: 245 persons per sq km

Settlement
% Urban population: 90
Main towns: London, Birmingham, Leeds, Glasgow

Land use
Main crops: Wheat, barley
Main industries: Food products, machinery, transport equipment, chemicals

Development indicators
Life expectancy: male 75, female 80
GNI per capita: US$ 25 250
Primary school enrolment ratio: 99
% Access to safe water: 100

Conic Equidistant projection

ENGLAND
WALES
UNITED KINGDOM
NORTHERN IRELAND
REPUBLIC OF IRELAND
FRANCE

Pennines
Cambrian Mountains
North York Moors
High Peak
Lake District
Brecon Beacons
Cotswold Hills
South Downs
The Weald
Mendip Hills
Dartmoor
Exmoor
Salisbury Plain
Wicklow Mts
Mourne Mts
Knockmealdown Mts
Slieve Bloom Mts

Scafell Pike 977
Snowdon 1085
Slieve Donard 852
Carrantuohill 1041

Irish Sea
English Channel
Bristol Channel
St George's Channel
Cardigan Bay
Lyme Bay
The Wash
Morecambe Bay
Galway Bay
Donegal Bay
Dundalk Bay
Caernarfon Bay
Colwyn Bay
Ebbw Vale

London, Birmingham, Manchester, Liverpool, Leeds, Cardiff, Dublin, Belfast

Land's End
Lizard Point
Hartland Point
Bill of Portland
Isle of Wight
Isle of Man
Isles of Scilly
Channel Islands
Alderney, Guernsey, Jersey, Sark
Aran Islands
Achill Island

United Kingdom

SCOTLAND

ENGLAND

WALES

NORTHERN
IRELAND

REPUBLIC
OF
IRELAND

London

Cardiff

Edinburgh

Belfast

Key

	International boundary
	National boundary
	Administrative boundary
	Capital city
o	Administrative centre

Scale 1 : 3 000 000

0   25   50   75   100 km

N
W   E
S

SHETLAND

Lerwick

ORKNEY

Kirkwall

WESTERN
ISLES

Stornoway

HIGHLAND

Inverness

MORAY

Elgin

ABERDEEN-
SHIRE

ABERDEEN

Aberdeen

SCOTLAND

ANGUS

Forfar

DUNDEE

Dundee

PERTH &
KINROSS

Perth

FIFE

Glenrothes

EAST
LOTHIAN

Haddington

Edinburgh

Dalkeith
MIDLOTHIAN

Livingston

STIRLING

Stirling

Falkirk

Kirkintilloch

Alloa

SCOTTISH
BORDERS

Newtown
St Boswells

ARGYLL
AND
BUTE

Lochgilphead

Dumbarton

Paisley
RENFREWSHIRE

Glasgow

Hamilton

Motherwell

SOUTH
LANARKSHIRE

NORTH
AYRSHIRE

Irvine

Ayr

EAST
AYRSHIRE

Kilmarnock

SOUTH
AYRSHIRE

NORTHUMBERLAND

MOYLE

Ballycastle

Coleraine

SCOTLAND
1. INVERCLYDE
2. WEST DUNBARTONSHIRE
3. EAST RENFREWSHIRE
4. GLASGOW CITY
5. EAST DUNBARTONSHIRE
6. NORTH LANARKSHIRE
7. FALKIRK
8. CLACKMANNANSHIRE
9. WEST LOTHIAN
10. EDINBURGH

NORTHERN IRELAND
1. NEWTOWNABBEY
2. CARRICKFERGUS
3. BELFAST
4. CASTLEREAGH
5. NORTH DOWN

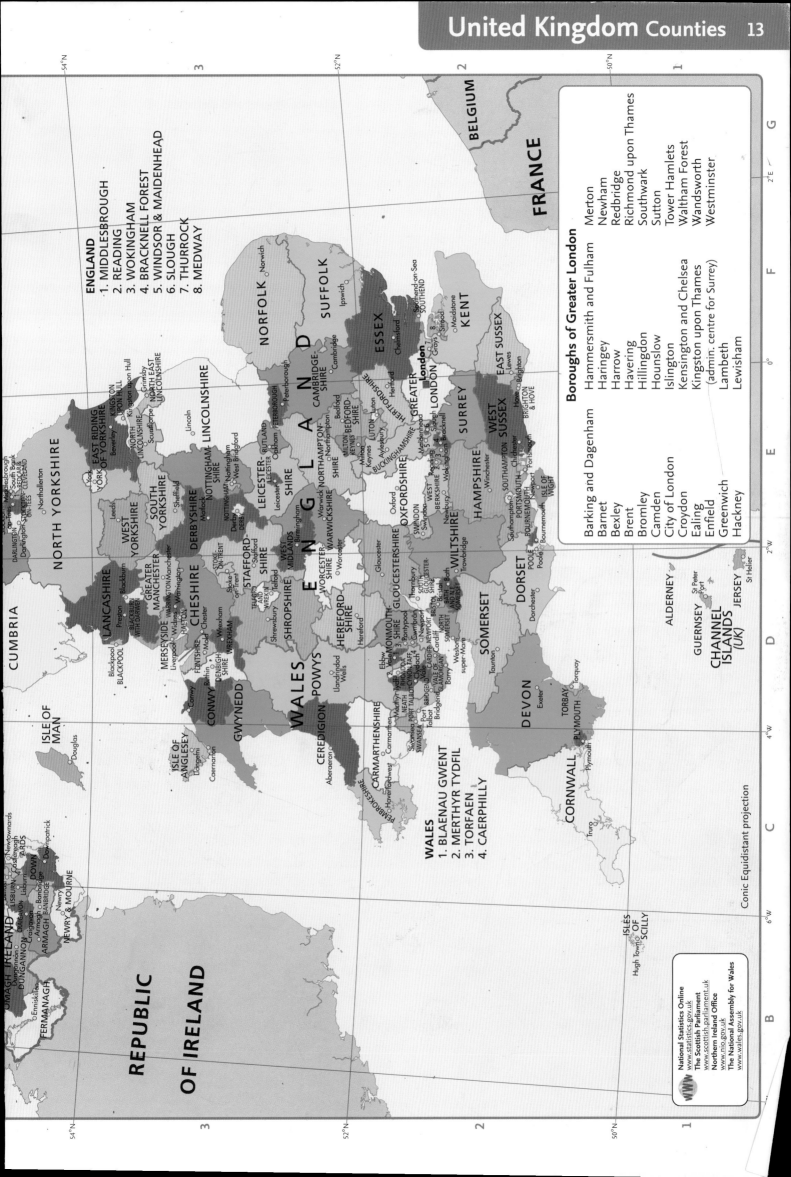

ENGLAND
1. MIDDLESBROUGH
2. READING
3. WOKINGHAM
4. BRACKNELL FOREST
5. WINDSOR & MAIDENHEAD
6. SLOUGH
7. THURROCK
8. MEDWAY

WALES
1. BLAENAU GWENT
2. MERTHYR TYDFIL
3. TORFAEN
4. CAERPHILLY

Boroughs of Greater London

Barking and Dagenham
Barnet
Bexley
Brent
Bromley
Camden
City of London
Croydon
Ealing
Enfield
Greenwich
Hackney
Hammersmith and Fulham
Haringey
Harrow
Havering
Hillingdon
Hounslow
Islington
Kensington and Chelsea
Kingston upon Thames
(admin. centre for Surrey)
Lambeth
Lewisham
Merton
Newham
Redbridge
Richmond upon Thames
Southwark
Sutton
Tower Hamlets
Waltham Forest
Wandsworth
Westminster

Conic Equidistant projection

National Statistics Online
www.statistics.gov.uk
The Scottish Parliament
www.scottish.parliament.uk
Northern Ireland Office
www.nio.gov.uk
The National Assembly for Wales
www.wales.gov.uk

Annual rainfall

There is little variation between winter and summer. The highest rainfall is in the west where winds from the sea blow against the mountains and hills. Central and eastern areas are more sheltered and have lower rainfall.

Average annual rainfall

- more than 2000 mm
- 1500 – 2000 mm
- 1000 – 1500 mm
- 750 – 1000 mm
- 625 – 750 mm
- less than 625 mm

- Location of places on climate graphs

Scale 1 : 10 000 000

WWW **Met Office**
www.metoffice.com
BBC Weather
www.bbc.co.uk/weather
UK Climate Impacts Programme
www.ukcip.org.uk

Climate graphs and statistics

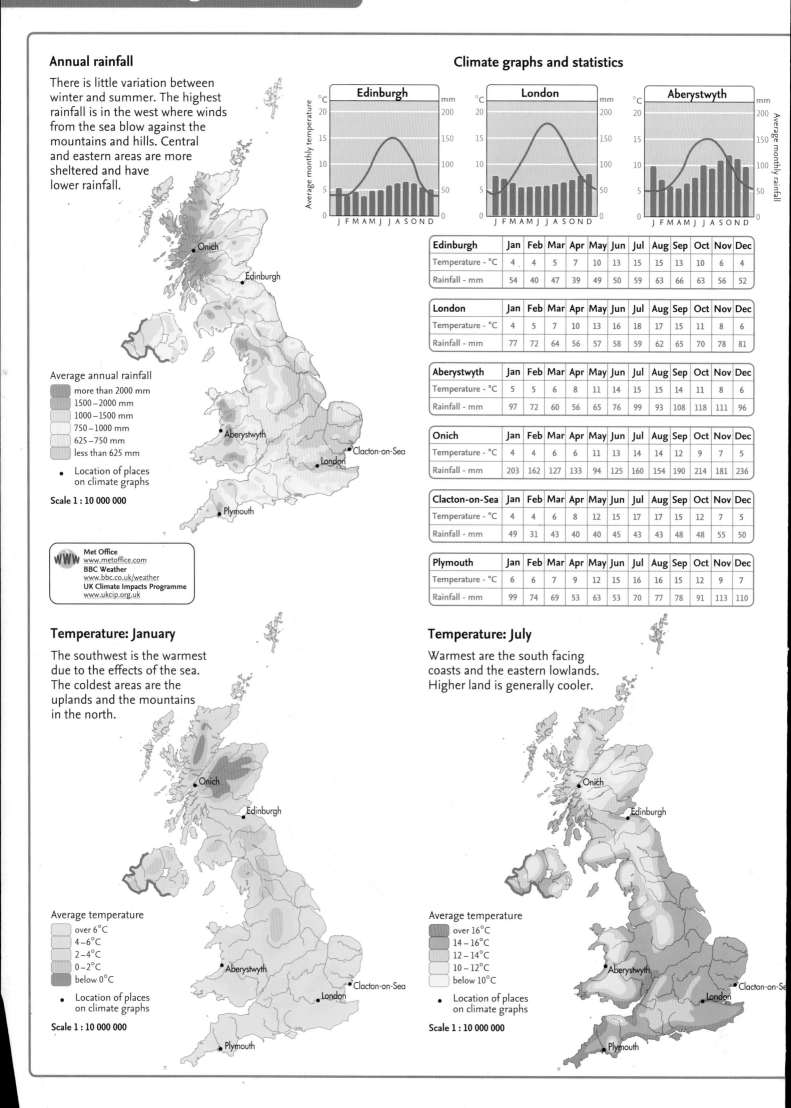

Edinburgh	Jan	Feb	Mar	Apr	May	Jun	Jul	Aug	Sep	Oct	Nov	Dec
Temperature - °C	4	4	5	7	10	13	15	15	13	10	6	4
Rainfall - mm	54	40	47	39	49	50	59	63	66	63	56	52

London	Jan	Feb	Mar	Apr	May	Jun	Jul	Aug	Sep	Oct	Nov	Dec
Temperature - °C	4	5	7	10	13	16	18	17	15	11	8	6
Rainfall - mm	77	72	64	56	57	58	59	62	65	70	78	81

Aberystwyth	Jan	Feb	Mar	Apr	May	Jun	Jul	Aug	Sep	Oct	Nov	Dec
Temperature - °C	5	5	6	8	11	14	15	15	14	11	8	6
Rainfall - mm	97	72	60	56	65	76	99	93	108	118	111	96

Onich	Jan	Feb	Mar	Apr	May	Jun	Jul	Aug	Sep	Oct	Nov	Dec
Temperature - °C	4	4	6	6	11	13	14	14	12	9	7	5
Rainfall - mm	203	162	127	133	94	125	160	154	190	214	181	236

Clacton-on-Sea	Jan	Feb	Mar	Apr	May	Jun	Jul	Aug	Sep	Oct	Nov	Dec
Temperature - °C	4	4	6	8	12	15	17	17	15	12	7	5
Rainfall - mm	49	31	43	40	40	45	43	43	48	48	55	50

Plymouth	Jan	Feb	Mar	Apr	May	Jun	Jul	Aug	Sep	Oct	Nov	Dec
Temperature - °C	6	6	7	9	12	15	16	16	15	12	9	7
Rainfall - mm	99	74	69	53	63	53	70	77	78	91	113	110

Temperature: January

The southwest is the warmest due to the effects of the sea. The coldest areas are the uplands and the mountains in the north.

Average temperature
- over 6°C
- 4 – 6°C
- 2 – 4°C
- 0 – 2°C
- below 0°C

- Location of places on climate graphs

Scale 1 : 10 000 000

Temperature: July

Warmest are the south facing coasts and the eastern lowlands. Higher land is generally cooler.

Average temperature
- over 16°C
- 14 – 16°C
- 12 – 14°C
- 10 – 12°C
- below 10°C

- Location of places on climate graphs

Scale 1 : 10 000 000

This is an image of central London that uses false colours. These colours are used to highlight important features. So for example the river Thames stands out as a purple line. The Thames flows from Barnes in the south western corner to Docklands in the north eastern corner. This satellite image covers an area of 250 sq km.

1 The rectangular black areas are the old London Docks. This is where ships used to be unloaded. Modern ships are too big for these docks which closed in 1981. Now the whole area is being redeveloped as part of Docklands.

2 The large bends on the river are called meanders. The area inside this meander is called the Isle of Dogs.

3 The centre of London is shown as a large pale purple patch. You can see the road and rail bridges which cross the river Thames.

4 These are the Houses of Parliament.

5 This is Buckingham Palace, with the Palace Gardens, Green Park and St James Park shown in green.

6 The green colours on the image are the parks and open spaces of London. Hyde Park stands out very clearly, with the Serpentine Lake in black. North of this is Regent's Park also shown in green.

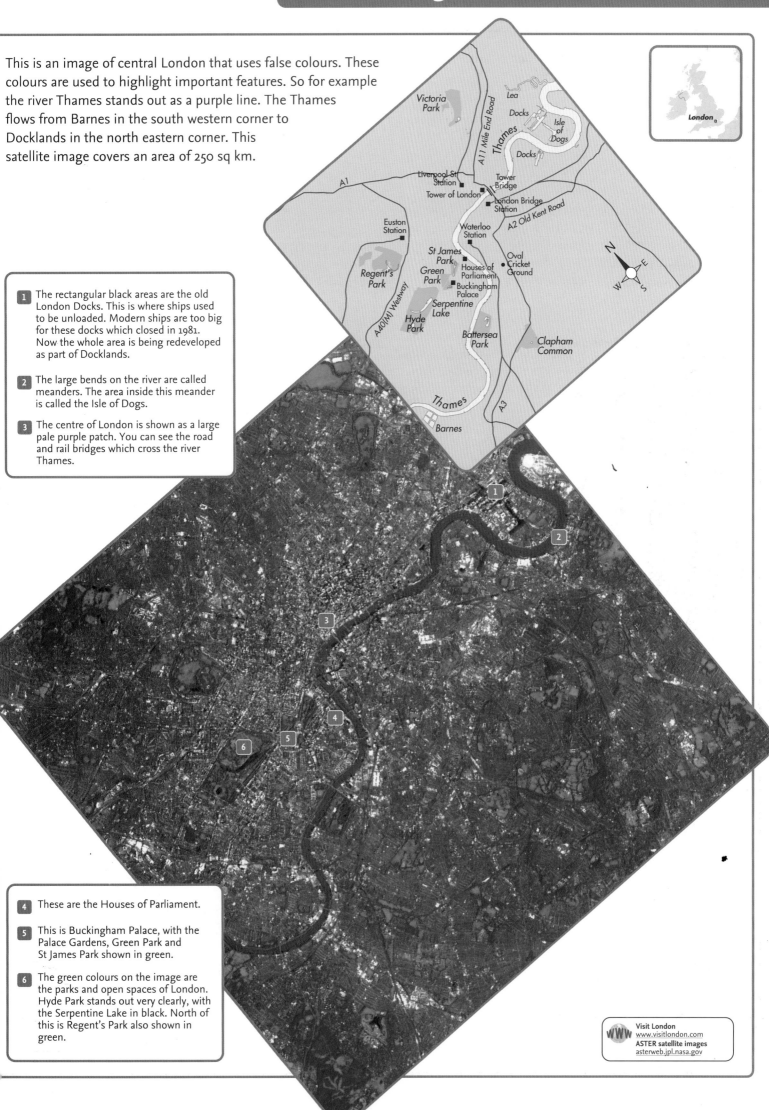

London

Victoria Park
Lea
Docks
Isle of Dogs
Thames
Docks
A11 Mile End Road
A1
Liverpool St Station
Tower Bridge
Tower of London
London Bridge Station
A2 Old Kent Road
Euston Station
Waterloo Station
St James Park
Green Park
Houses of Parliament
Oval Cricket Ground
Regent's Park
Buckingham Palace
Serpentine Lake
A40(M) Westway
Hyde Park
Battersea Park
Clapham Common
Thames
A3
Barnes

N E S W

Key

- over 5000 m
- 3000 – 5000 m
- 2000 – 3000 m
- 1000 – 2000 m
- 500 – 1000 m
- 200 – 500 m
- 0 – 200 m
- land below sea level
- Ice cap
- ▲ 5642 Mountain height (in metres)

Scale 1 : 25 000 000

0   250   500   750   1000 km

Facts about Europe Relief

Area
9 908 599 sq km

Highest peak
El'brus 5642 m

Lowest point
Caspian Sea -28 m

Longest river
Volga 3 688 km

Largest lake
Caspian Sea 371 000 sq km

Conic Equidistant projection

A. ANDORRA
L. LIECHTENSTEIN
LUX. LUXEMBOURG
M. MONACO
NETH. NETHERLANDS
S.M. SAN MARINO

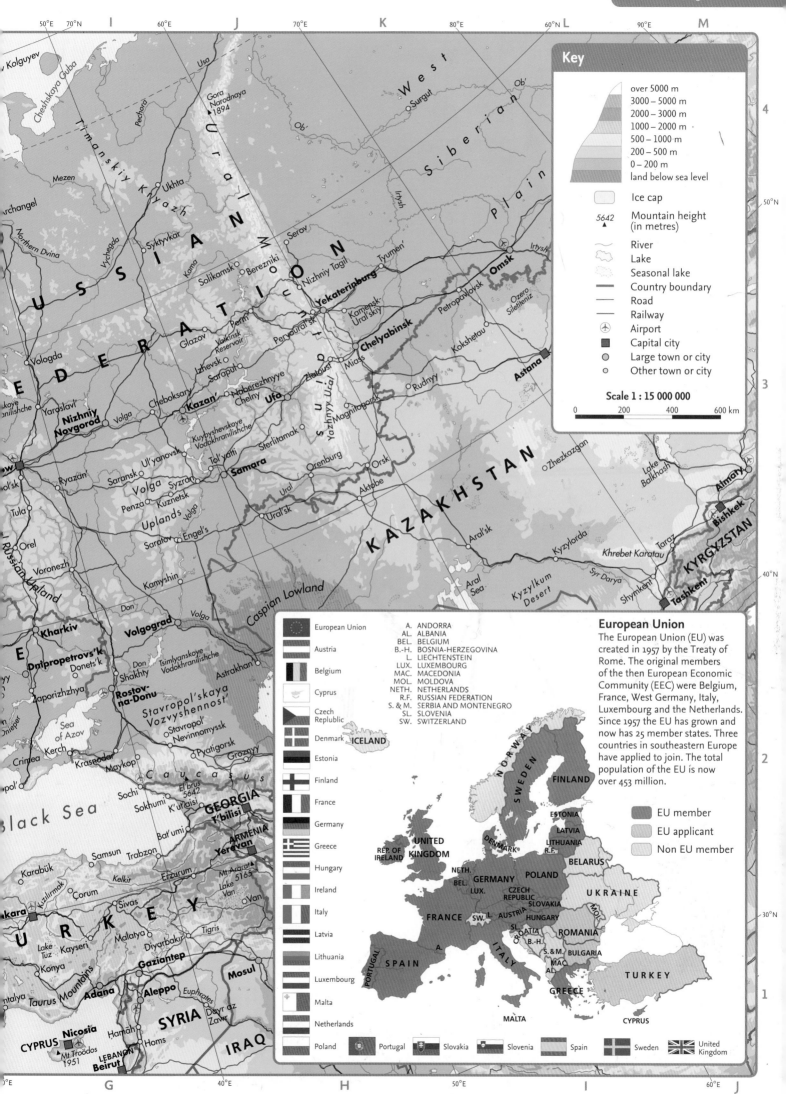

Conic Equidistant projection

GERMANY
Ulm
Augsburg
Linz
Munich
Danube
Colmar
Neckar
Memmingen
Rosenheim
Chiemsee
Burghausen
Mulhouse
Lake Constance
Kempten
Salzburg
Traunsee
Hochschwab 2277
Basel
Zürich
St Gallen
Zugspitze 2962
Garmisch-Partenkirchen
Innsbruck
Brenner Pass
Großglockner 3798
Liezen
Enns
Grosser Speikkogel 2140
Lucerne
Vaduz
LIECHTENSTEIN
AUSTRIA
Lienz
Karnische Alpen
Lake Neuchâtel
Bern
SWITZERLAND
Jungfrau 4158
Wildhorn
St Moritz
Piz Bernina 4049
Bolzano
3343
Trento
Dolomites
Udine
Drau
Klagenfurt
Ljubljana
Grosser Speikkogel
Snežnik 1796
Kupa

Lausanne
Lake Geneva
Geneva
Chamonix-Mont-Blanc
4808 Mont Blanc
Chambéry
Gran Paradiso 4061
Matterhorn 4478
Monte Rosa 4634
Great St Bernard Pass
Aosta
Simplon Pass
Lake Maggiore
Lugano
Lake Como
Adda
Monza
Bergamo
Lake Garda
Verona
Vicenza
Padua
Piave
Venice
Gulf of Venice
Trieste
Istria
SLOVENIA
Rijeka
Pula
Cres
CROATIA

FRANCE
Grenoble
Gap
Durance
Mont Blanc
Mt Pelat 3051
Maritime Alps
Sisteron
Cuneo
Monte Viso 3841
Tanaro
Novara
Milan
Turin
Piacenza
Alessandria
Monte Maggiorasca 1799
Parma
Reggio nell'Emilia
Oglio
Po
Mantua
Adige
Ferrara
Modena
Reno
Bologna
Forlì
Rimini
Pag
Vaganski Vrh 1758
Zadar
BOSNIA-HERZEGOVINA
Knin
Ploćno 2228
Sarajevo
Dugi Otok
Dalmatia
Mostar
Durmitor 252

MONACO
San Remo
Monte-Carlo
Cannes
Nice
Côte d'Azur
Toulon
To Spain
To Marseille
Albenga
Gulf of Genoa
Genoa
La Spezia
Ligurian Sea
Pisa
Livorno
Arno
Florence
Siena
San Marino
SAN MARINO
Ancona
Adriatic Sea
Split
Brač
Vis
Hvar
Korčula
Mljet
Dubrovnik
Nikšić

Cap Corse
Isola di Capraia
Isola d'Elba
Isola Pianosa
Perugia
Lago Trasimeno
Tolentino
Monte Vettore 2476
Tiber
Terni
2216
Monte Corno 2912
Pescara
Pescara
Termoli

Corsica (France)
Calvi
Bastia
Monte Cinto 2706
Corte
Ajaccio
Golfe de Valinco
Isola Pianosa
Isola di Montecristo
Lago di Bolsena
Viterbo
Civitavecchia
Monte Terminillo
L'Aquila
Monte Corno
Monte Velino 2487
ITALY
Monte Greco 2283
Foggia
Bari

Bonifacio
Strait of Bonifacio
Isola Caprera
Golfo dell'Asinara
Porto Torres
Punta Balestrieri 1359
Olbia
Sassari
Nuoro
Golfo di Orosei
Rome
Tivoli
Latina
Pontine Islands
Golfo di Gaeta
Naples
Vesuvius
Isola d'Ischia
Salerno
Potenza
Ofanto
Bradano
Brindisi
Lecce
Otranto
To Greece
Taranto

Tyrrhenian Sea
Oristano
Capo della Frasca
Tirso
Punta La Marmora 1834
Capo di Monte Santu
Sardinia (Italy)
Nuoro
Isola di Capri
Golfo di Salerno
Sapri
Golfo di Policastro
Monte Pollino 2248
Corigliano Calabro
Gulf of Taranto
Capo Santa Maria di Leuca

Iglesias
Isola di San Pietro
Cagliari
Golfo di Cagliari
Capo Carbonara
Capo Spartivento
Cosenza
Monte Botte Donato 1928
Catanzaro
Ionian Sea

Isola di Ustica
Isola di Stromboli
Isole Lipari
Messina
Reggio di Calabria
Capo Spartivento

To Tunisia
Palermo
Trapani
Rocca Busambra 1613
Monti Nebrodi 1847
Mount Etna 3323
Sicily
Caltanissetta
Catania
Syracuse

To Tunisia
Agrigento
Mediterranean Sea
Isola di Pantelleria (Italy)
Capo Passero
Gozo
Isola di Linosa (Italy)
Valletta
MALTA

Facts about Italy

Landscape
Area: 301 245 sq km
Highest point: Mont Blanc 4808 m

Population
Total: 57 423 000
Density: 191 persons per sq km

Settlement
% Urban population: 67
Main towns: Rome, Milan, Naples, Turin

Land use
Main crops: Sugar beets, corn, grapes
Main industries: Machinery, metal products, chemicals, food

Development indicators
Life expectancy: male 75, female 81
GNP per capita: US$ 18 960
Primary school enrolment ratio: 100
% Access to safe water: 100

Key

over 5000 m
3000 – 5000 m
2000 – 3000 m
1000 – 2000 m
500 – 1000 m
200 – 500 m
0 – 200 m
land below sea level
4808 ▲ Mountain height (in metres)
Ice cap

～～ River
Lake
Country boundary
Road
Railway
✈ Airport
■ Capital city
● Large town or city
○ Other town or city

Scale 1 : 5 250 000

0   50   100   150   200 km

N
W E
S

Lambert Conformal Conic project

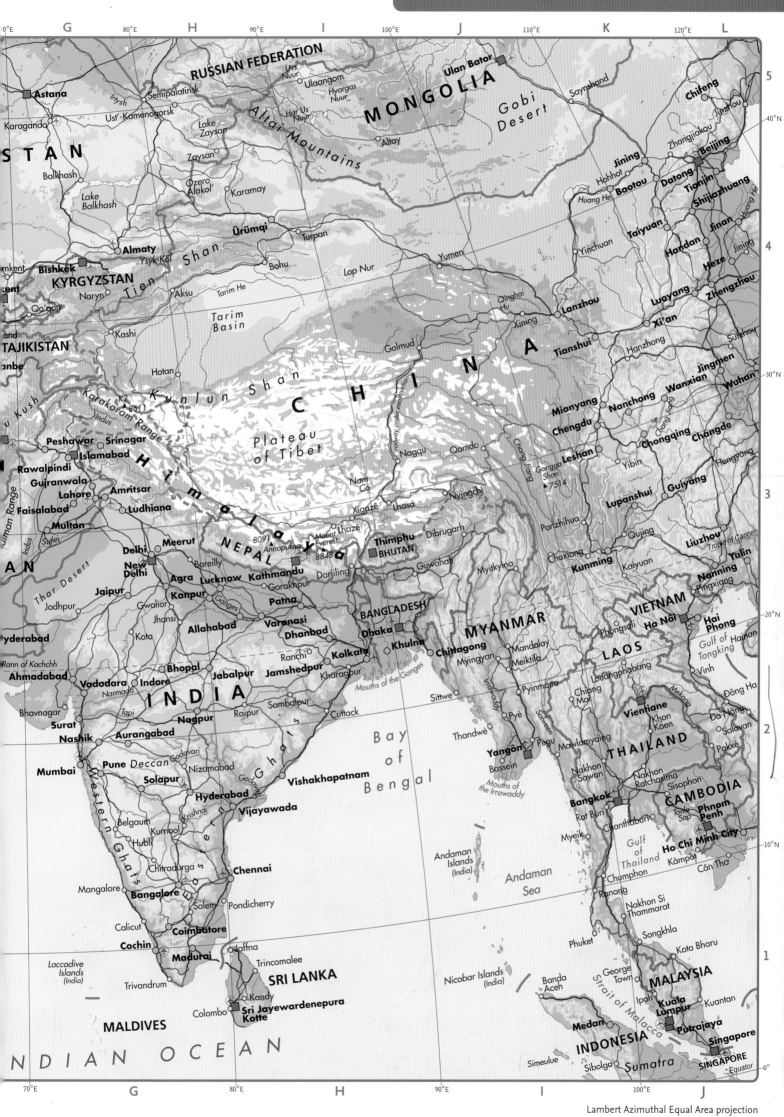

Lambert Azimuthal Equal Area projection

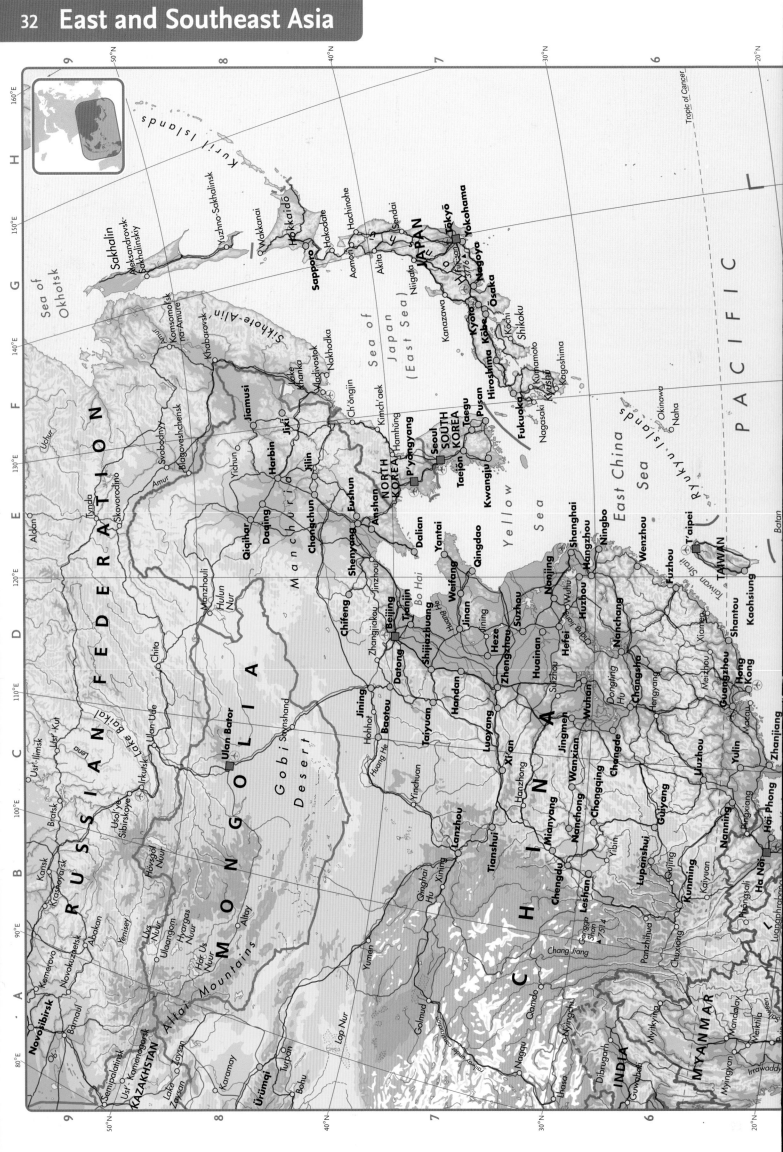

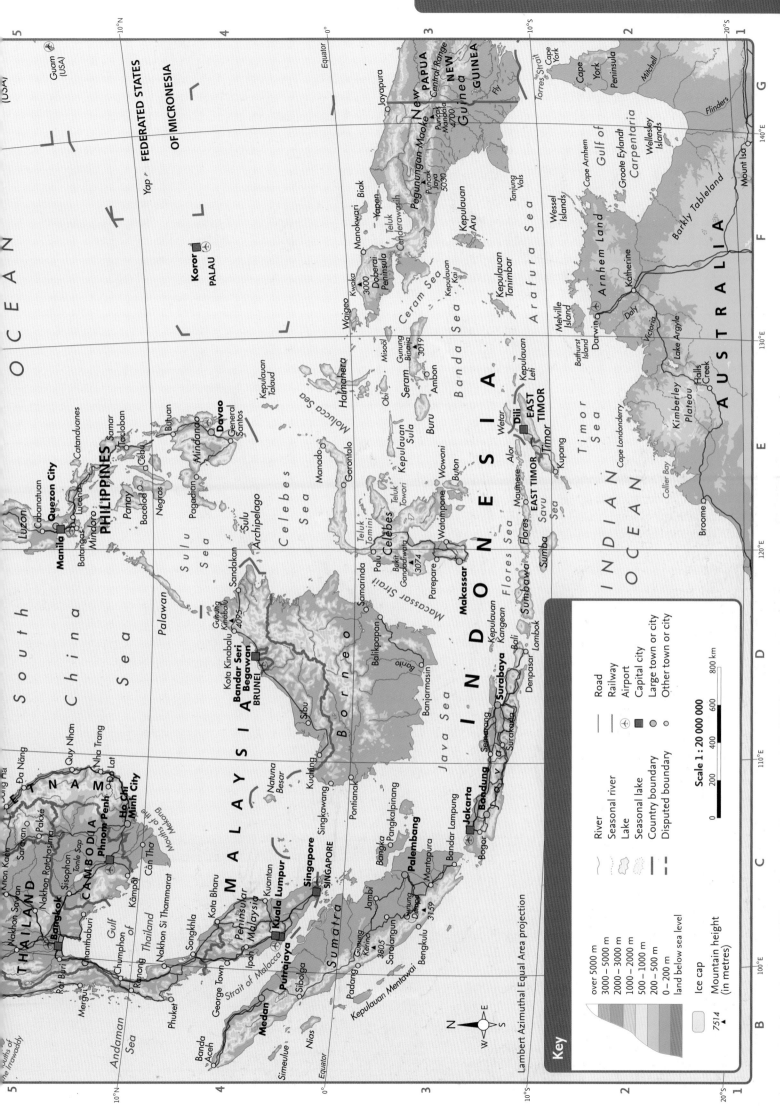

Key

Road
Railway
Airport
Capital city
Large town or city
Other town or city

River
Seasonal river
Lake
Seasonal lake
Country boundary
Disputed boundary

Scale 1 : 20 000 000

0   200   400   600   800 km

over 5000 m
3000 – 5000 m
2000 – 3000 m
1000 – 2000 m
500 – 1000 m
200 – 500 m
0 – 200 m
land below sea level

Ice cap

7514 ▲ Mountain height (in metres)

Lambert Azimuthal Equal Area projection

Facts about Japan

Landscape
Area: 377 727 sq km
Highest point: Fuji-san 3776 m

Population
Total: 127 654 000
Density: 338 persons per sq km

Settlement
% Urban population: 79
Main towns: Tōkyō, Ōsaka-Kōbe,
Nagoya, Fukuoka-Kita-Kyūshū

Land use
Main crops: Rice, potatoes, sugar beets
Main industries: Electrical equipment,
transport equipment, other machinery,
chemicals

Development indicators
Life expectancy: male 77, female 85
GNP per capita: US$ 33 550
Primary school enrolment ratio: 101
% Access to safe water: 100

Key

3000 – 5000 m	
2000 – 3000 m	
1000 – 2000 m	
500 – 1000 m	
200 – 500 m	
0 – 200 m	

3776 ▲ Mountain height (in metres)

~~~ River
Lake

—— Country boundary
- - - Disputed boundary
—— Road
—— Railway
········ Ferry
⊕ Airport
■ Capital city
◉ Large town or city
○ Other town or city

Japanese name forms
-dake	peak
-hanto	peninsula
-jima	island
-kai	bay, inlet
-kaikyo	strait
-ko	lake
-nada	sea, gulf
-retto	chain of islands
-san	mountain
-sanchi	mountainous area
-shima	island
-suido	strait, channel
-to	island
-wan	sea
-yama	mountain

Scale 1 : 7 500 000

0   100   200   300   400 km

Albers Equal Area Conic projection

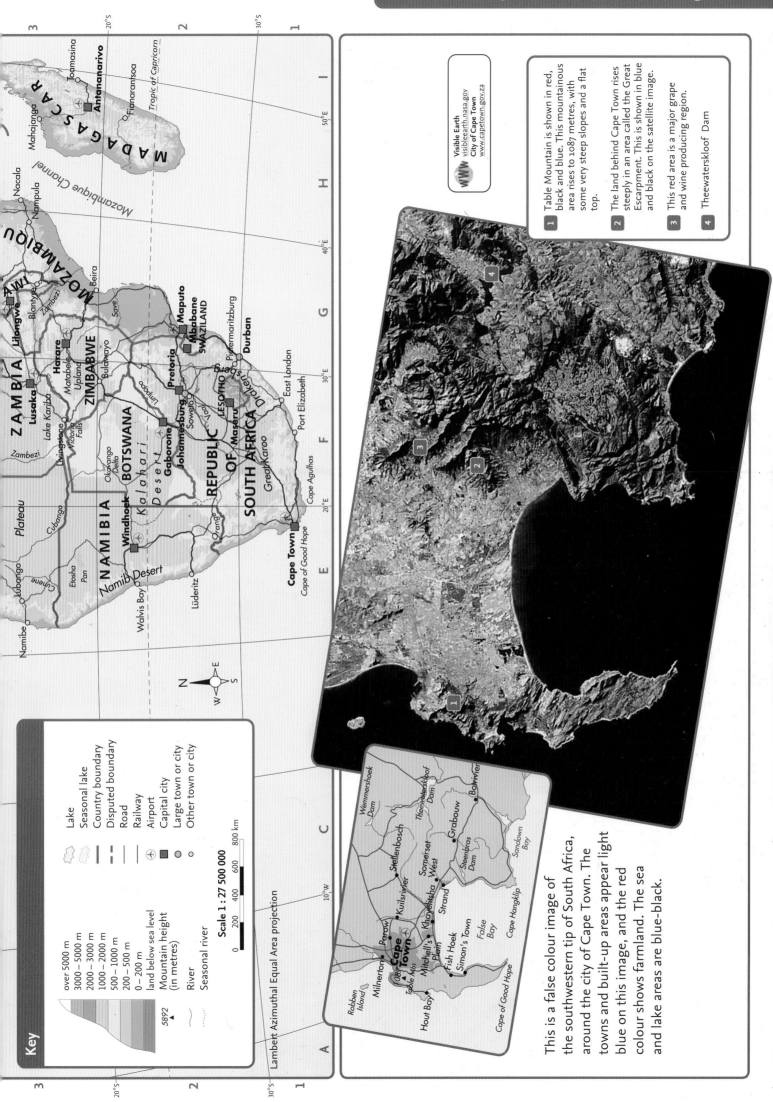

Key

over 5000 m	
3000 – 5000 m	
2000 – 3000 m	
1000 – 2000 m	
500 – 1000 m	
200 – 500 m	
0 – 200 m	
land below sea level	

5892 ▲ Mountain height (in metres)

River
Seasonal river

Lake
Seasonal lake
Country boundary
Disputed boundary
Road
Railway
⊕ Airport
■ Capital city
● Large town or city
○ Other town or city

Scale 1 : 27 500 000

0   200   400   600   800 km

Lambert Azimuthal Equal Area projection

This is a false colour image of the southwestern tip of South Africa, around the city of Cape Town. The towns and built-up areas appear light blue on this image, and the red colour shows farmland. The sea and lake areas are blue-black.

Visible Earth
visibleearth.nasa.gov
City of Cape Town
www.capetown.gov.za

1 Table Mountain is shown in red, black and blue. This mountainous area rises to 1087 metres, with some very steep slopes and a flat top.

2 The land behind Cape Town rises steeply in an area called the Great Escarpment. This is shown in blue and black on the satellite image.

3 This red area is a major grape and wine producing region.

4 Theewaterskloof Dam

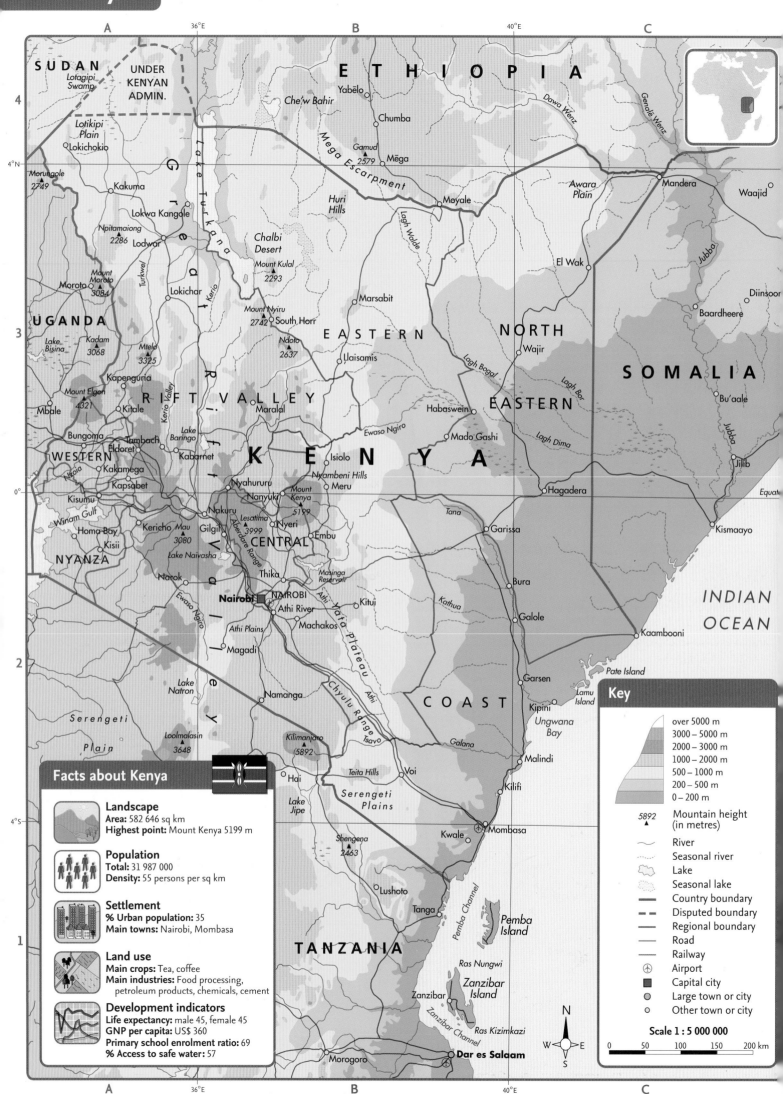

SUDAN
Lotagipi Swamp
UNDER KENYAN ADMIN.
Lotikipi Plain
Lokichokio
Morungole 2749
Kakuma
Lokwa Kangole
Npitamaiong 2286 Lodwar
Moroto
Mount Moroto 3084
Lokichar

ETHIOPIA
Yabēlo
Che'w Bahir
Chumba
Mega Escarpment
Gamud 2579 Mēga
Moyale
Dawa Wenz
Genale Wenz

Huri Hills
Chalbi Desert
Mount Kulal 2293

Awara Plain
Mandera
Waajid

El Wak
Diinsoor
Baardheere

Lake Turkana
Great

UGANDA
Lake Bisina
Kadam 3068
Mbale
Mount Elgon 4321
Kapenguria
Kitale
Mtelo 3325

Turkwel *Kerio*
Lokichar

Mount Nyiru 2742 South Horr
Ndoto 2637
Marsabit
Llaisamis

EASTERN

NORTH
Lagh Walde
Wajir

SOMALIA
Bu'aale
Jubba
Jilib

EASTERN
Lagh Bogal
Habaswein
Lagh Bor
Lagh Dima
Mado Gashi
Hagadera

RIFT VALLEY
WESTERN
Bungoma
Tambach
Eldoret
Kakamega
Kapsabet
Nzoia
Kisumu
Winam Gulf
Homa Bay
Kisii
NYANZA

Maralal
Lake Baringo
Kabarnet
Kerio
KENYA

Isiolo
Nyambeni Hills
Meru
Nyahururu
Nanyuki
Mount Kenya 5199
Nyeri
Aberdare Range
Lesatima 3999
Gilgil
Nakuru
Kericho
Mau 3080
Lake Naivasha
CENTRAL
Embu

Ewaso Ngiro

Tana
Garissa
Kathua
Bura
Galole

Kaambooni

INDIAN OCEAN

Narok
Thika
Nairobi NAIROBI
Athi River
Athi Plains
Machakos
Kitui
Athi
Yatta Plateau

Ewaso Ngiro
Magadi
Chyulu Range
Tsavo

Lake Natron
Serengeti Plain
Loolmalasin 3648
Namanga
Kilimanjaro 5892
Hai

Garsen
Galana
Pate Island
Lamu Island
Ungwana Bay
Kipini

Teita Hills
Voi
COAST
Malindi
Kilifi

Shengena 2463
Kwale
Mombasa

Lushoto
Serengeti Plains
Lake Jipe

TANZANIA
Tanga
Pemba Channel
Pemba Island
Ras Nungwi
Zanzibar Island
Zanzibar
Zanzibar Channel
Ras Kizimkazi
Morogoro
Dar es Salaam

Facts about Kenya

Landscape
Area: 582 646 sq km
Highest point: Mount Kenya 5199 m

Population
Total: 31 987 000
Density: 55 persons per sq km

Settlement
% Urban population: 35
Main towns: Nairobi, Mombasa

Land use
Main crops: Tea, coffee
Main industries: Food processing, petroleum products, chemicals, cement

Development indicators
Life expectancy: male 45, female 45
GNP per capita: US$ 360
Primary school enrolment ratio: 69
% Access to safe water: 57

Key

over 5000 m
3000 – 5000 m
2000 – 3000 m
1000 – 2000 m
500 – 1000 m
200 – 500 m
0 – 200 m

5892 ▲ Mountain height (in metres)
River
Seasonal river
Lake
Seasonal lake
Country boundary
Disputed boundary
Regional boundary
Road
Railway
⊕ Airport
■ Capital city
● Large town or city
○ Other town or city

Scale 1 : 5 000 000
0   50   100   150   200 km

Lambert Azimuthal Equal Area projecti

Masai Mara National Reserve

Situated on the border with Tanzania, the Masai Mara National Reserve is one of Kenya's best known wildlife reserves. Animals such as gazelles, elephants, cheetahs, buffalo and a few black rhino live here all year round. During July and October over one million wildebeest and a quarter of a million zebra move through the Masai Mara on their migrations from and to the Serengeti in Tanzania.

WWW Game Reserve.com
www.game-reserve.com

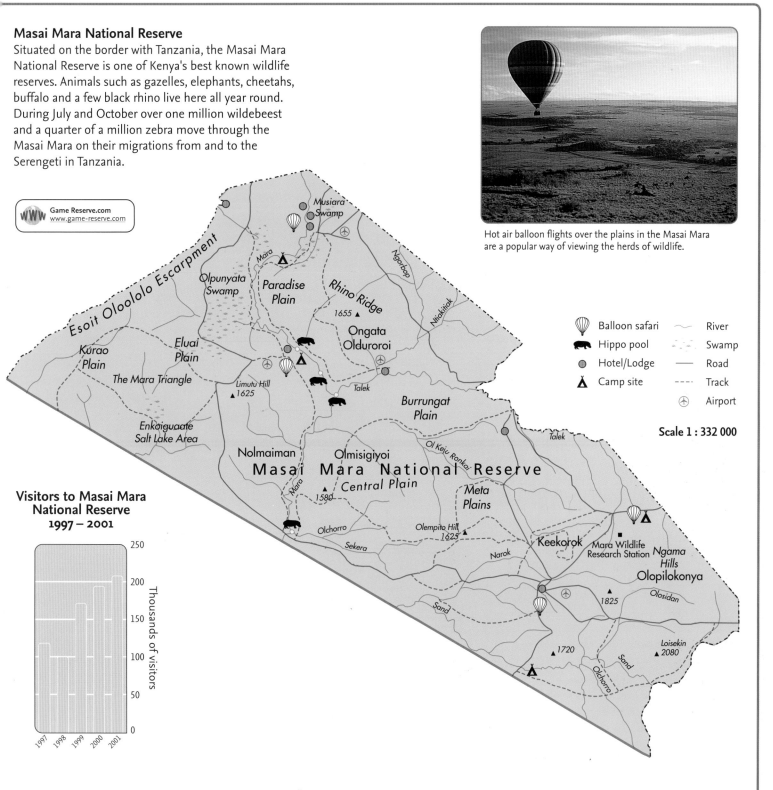

Hot air balloon flights over the plains in the Masai Mara are a popular way of viewing the herds of wildlife.

Legend:
- Balloon safari
- Hippo pool
- Hotel/Lodge
- Camp site
- River
- Swamp
- Road
- Track
- Airport

Scale 1 : 332 000

Visitors to Masai Mara National Reserve
1997 – 2001

(Bar chart: Thousands of visitors, 0–250, years 1997, 1998, 1999, 2000, 2001)

Africa's top tourist destinations 2002

Rank	Country	Visitors
1	South Africa	6 550 000
2	Tunisia	5 506 000
3	Egypt	4 906 000
4	Morocco	4 193 000
5	Botswana	1 037 000
6	Algeria	998 000
7	Kenya	838 000
8	Mauritius	682 000
9	Zambia	565 000
10	Tanzania	550 000
11	Ghana	483 000

For four months every year herds of wildebeest from Tanzania graze on the Mara plains. Tall grasses are reduced to stubble before the herds trek south again.

Hippos can be found wallowing in pools in the Mara river.

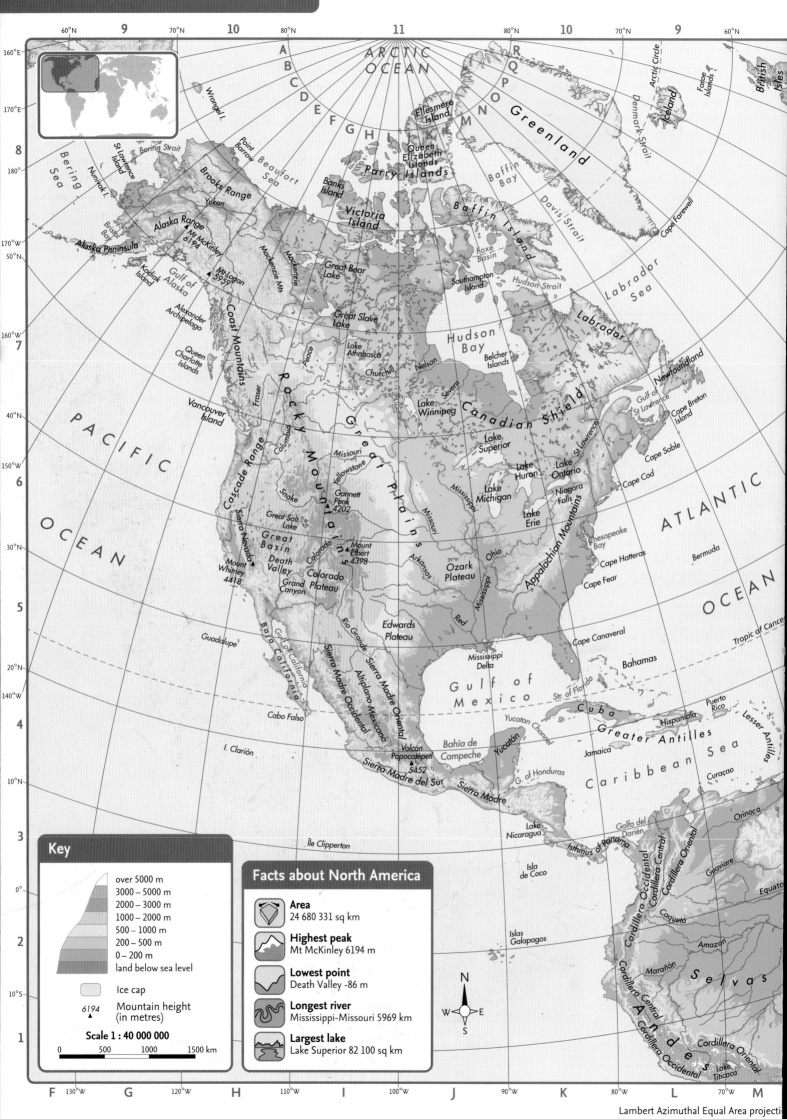

ARCTIC OCEAN

Wrangel I.
Point Barrow
Beaufort Sea
Bering Strait
Bering Sea
St Lawrence Island
Nunivak I.
Brooks Range
Yukon
Alaska Range
Mt McKinley 6194
Mt Logan 5959
Alaska Peninsula
Gulf of Alaska
Kodiak Island
Alexander Archipelago
Coast Mountains
Queen Charlotte Islands
Vancouver Island
Mackenzie Mts
Mackenzie
Great Bear Lake
Great Slave Lake
Lake Athabasca
Peace
Churchill
Nelson
Banks Island
Victoria Island
Parry Islands
Queen Elizabeth Islands
Ellesmere Island
Baffin Bay
Baffin Island
Foxe Basin
Southampton Island
Hudson Strait
Belcher Islands
Hudson Bay
Severn
Canadian Shield
Labrador
Labrador Sea
Newfoundland
Gulf of St Lawrence
Cape Breton Island
Cape Farewell
Denmark Strait
Greenland
Arctic Circle
Iceland
Faroe Islands
British Isles

PACIFIC OCEAN

Rocky Mountains
Cascade Range
Fraser
Columbia
Snake
Sierra Nevada
Great Salt Lake
Great Basin
Death Valley
Mount Whitney 4418
Grand Canyon
Colorado Plateau
Colorado
Mount Elbert 4398
Yellowstone
Gannett Peak 4202
Missouri
Great Plains
Lake Winnipeg
Lake Superior
Lake Michigan
Lake Huron
Lake Erie
Lake Ontario
Niagara Falls
St Lawrence
Mississippi
Missouri
Ozark Plateau
Arkansas
Ohio
Red
Appalachian Mountains
Chesapeake Bay
Cape Cod
Cape Sable
Cape Hatteras
Cape Fear
Cape Canaveral
ATLANTIC OCEAN
Bermuda

Guadalupe
Baja California
Gulf of California
Cabo Falso
I. Clarión
Rio Grande
Sierra Madre Occidental
Altiplano Mexicano
Sierra Madre Oriental
Edwards Plateau
Mississippi Delta
Gulf of Mexico
Str. of Florida
Bahamas
Tropic of Cancer
Cuba
Greater Antilles
Hispaniola
Puerto Rico
Lesser Antilles
Jamaica
Curaçao
Caribbean Sea

Île Clipperton
Volcán Popocatépetl 5452
Bahía de Campeche
Yucatán
Yucatán Channel
G. of Honduras
Sierra Madre del Sur
Sierra Madre
Lake Nicaragua
Isla de Coco
Isthmus of Panama
Golfo del Darién
Cordillera Occidental
Cordillera Central
Cordillera Oriental
Guaviare
Orinoco
Equator
Caquetá
Marañón
Amazon
Selvas
Andes
Cordillera Central
Cordillera Oriental
Cordillera Occidental
Lake Titicaca
Islas Galapagos

60°N 9 70°N 10 80°N 11 80°N 10 70°N 9 60°N
160°E
170°E
180°
170°W 50°N
160°W
150°W
140°W
130°W F 120°W G 110°W H 100°W I 90°W J 80°W K 70°W L M
8, 7, 6, 5, 4, 3, 2, 1

A B C D E F G H I J K L M N O P Q R

Key

- over 5000 m
- 3000 – 5000 m
- 2000 – 3000 m
- 1000 – 2000 m
- 500 – 1000 m
- 200 – 500 m
- 0 – 200 m
- land below sea level
- Ice cap
- 6194 ▲ Mountain height (in metres)

Scale 1 : 40 000 000

0   500   1000   1500 km

Facts about North America

Area
24 680 331 sq km

Highest peak
Mt McKinley 6194 m

Lowest point
Death Valley -86 m

Longest river
Mississippi-Missouri 5969 km

Largest lake
Lake Superior 82 100 sq km

N
W   E
S

Lambert Azimuthal Equal Area projection

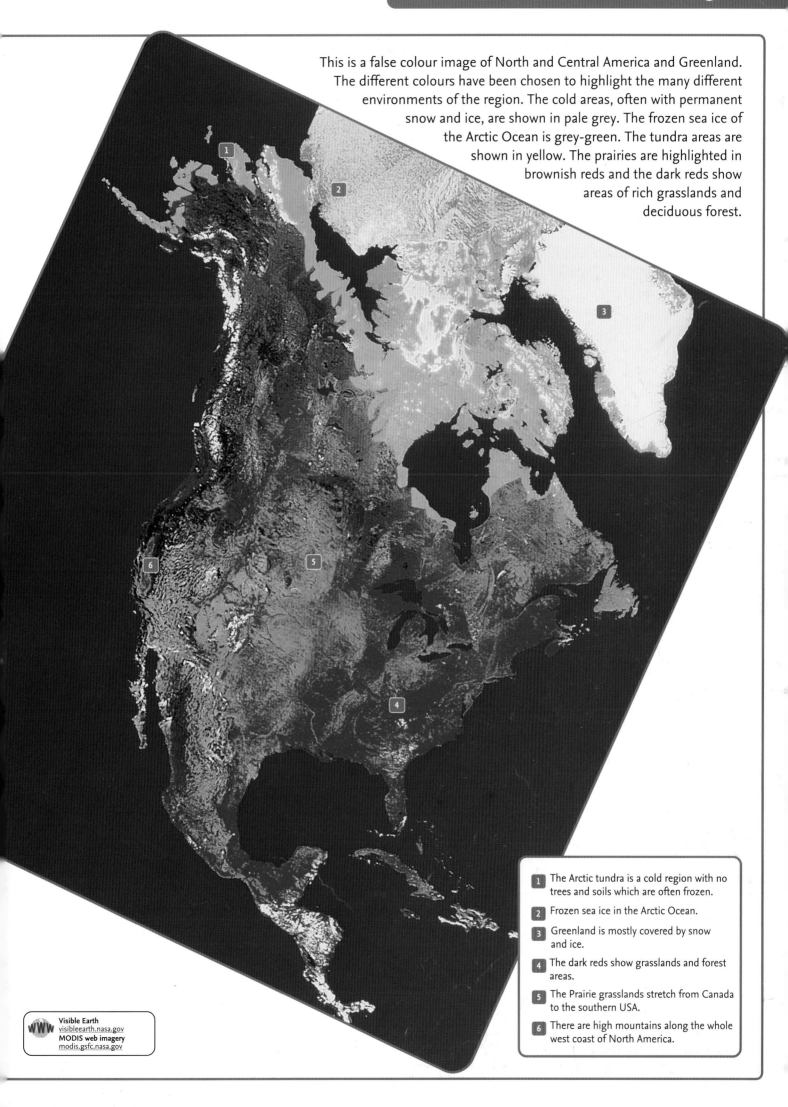

This is a false colour image of North and Central America and Greenland. The different colours have been chosen to highlight the many different environments of the region. The cold areas, often with permanent snow and ice, are shown in pale grey. The frozen sea ice of the Arctic Ocean is grey-green. The tundra areas are shown in yellow. The prairies are highlighted in brownish reds and the dark reds show areas of rich grasslands and deciduous forest.

1 The Arctic tundra is a cold region with no trees and soils which are often frozen.

2 Frozen sea ice in the Arctic Ocean.

3 Greenland is mostly covered by snow and ice.

4 The dark reds show grasslands and forest areas.

5 The Prairie grasslands stretch from Canada to the southern USA.

6 There are high mountains along the whole west coast of North America.

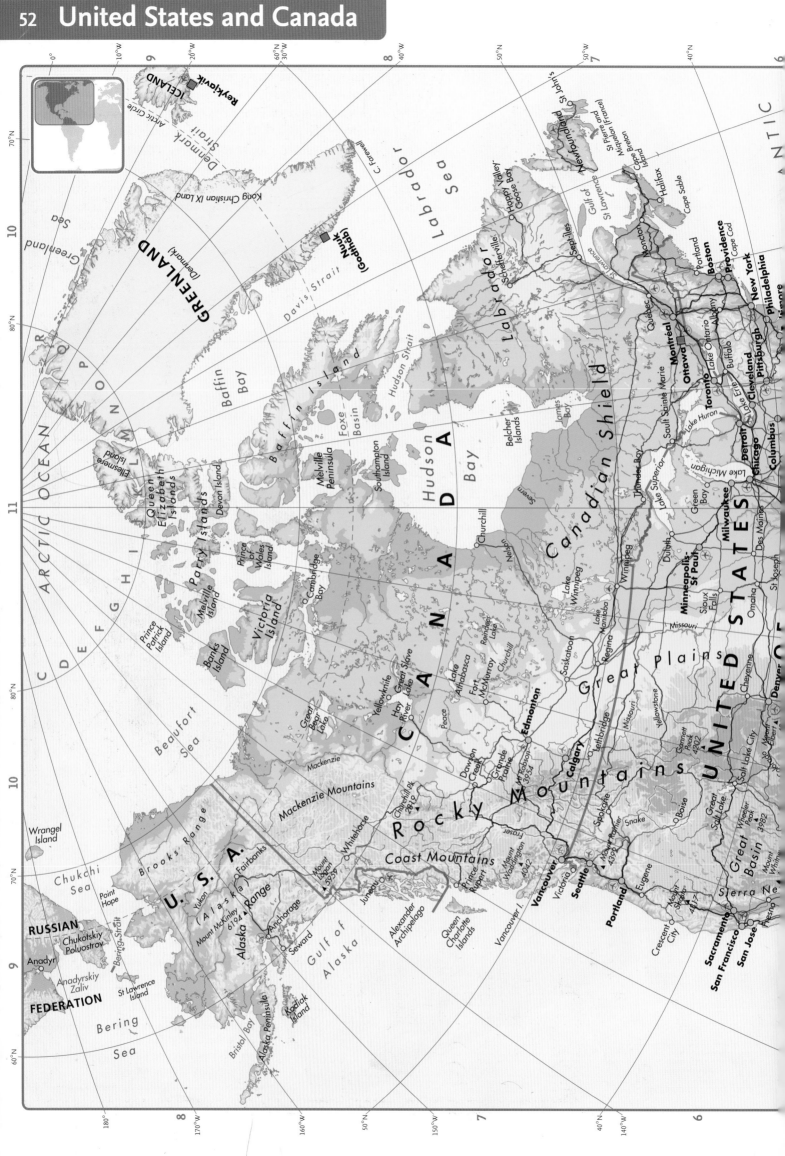

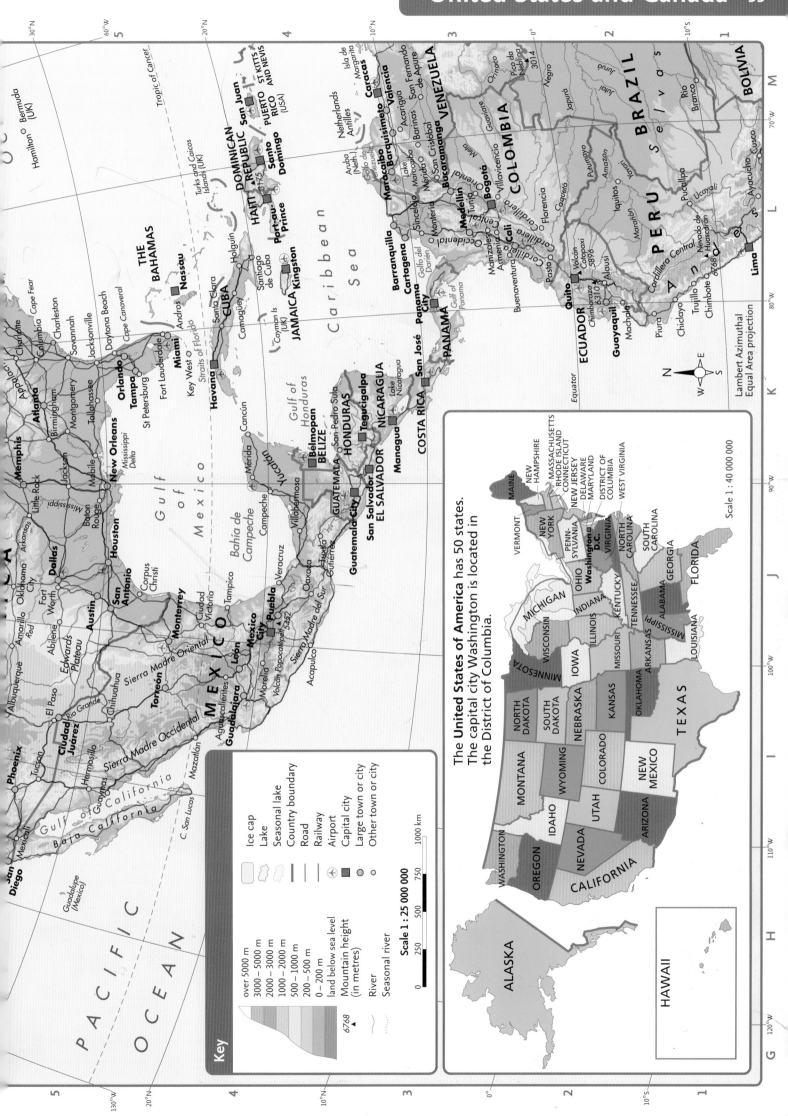

Key

- Ice cap
- Lake
- Seasonal lake
- Country boundary
- Road
- Railway
- ✈ Airport
- ■ Capital city
- ○ Large town or city
- ○ Other town or city

Scale 1 : 25 000 000

| over 5000 m |
| 3000 – 5000 m |
| 2000 – 3000 m |
| 1000 – 2000 m |
| 500 – 1000 m |
| 200 – 500 m |
| 0 – 200 m |
| land below sea level |

Mountain height (in metres)

▲ 6768

River

Seasonal river

0   250   500   750   1000 km

The United States of America has 50 states. The capital city Washington is located in the District of Columbia.

Scale 1 : 40 000 000

Lambert Azimuthal Equal Area projection

N E S W

PACIFIC OCEAN

Bermuda (UK)
Hamilton ○

Tropic of Cancer

THE BAHAMAS
Nassau ■
Andros
Santa Clara
CUBA
Holguín
Camagüey
Santiago de Cuba
Cayman Is (UK)
JAMAICA
Kingston

Turks and Caicos Islands (UK)

DOMINICAN REPUBLIC
HAITI
Port-au-Prince
Santo Domingo
PUERTO RICO (USA)
San Juan
ST KITTS AND NEVIS

Caribbean Sea

Netherlands Antilles
Aruba (Neth.)
Isla de Margarita
Caracas
Valencia
Barquisimeto
Maracaibo
VENEZUELA
San Fernando de Apure

Cape Fear
Charleston
Columbia
Charlotte
Savannah
Jacksonville
Daytona Beach
Cape Canaveral
Orlando
Tampa
St Petersburg
Fort Lauderdale
Miami
Key West
Straits of Florida
Havana

Atlanta
Montgomery
Birmingham
Tallahassee
Mobile
Jackson
New Orleans
Mississippi Delta

Memphis
Little Rock
Baton Rouge

Appalachian

Oklahoma City
Fort Worth
Dallas
Amarillo
Abilene
Edwards Plateau
San Antonio
Austin
Houston
Corpus Christi

Albuquerque
El Paso
Ciudad Juárez
Chihuahua
Hermosillo
Guaymas
Phoenix
Tucson

San Diego
Mexicali
Guadalupe (Mexico)
Baja California
Gulf of California

Rio Grande
Monterrey
Torreón
Aguascalientes
León
Guadalajara
MEXICO
Sierra Madre Occidental
Sierra Madre Oriental
Ciudad Victoria
Tampico
Mazatlán
Morelia
Mexico City
Puebla
Volcán Popocatépetl 5452
Acapulco
Sierra Madre del Sur
Oaxaca
Veracruz
Villahermosa
Tuxtla Gutiérrez
Campeche
Bahía de Campeche
Mérida
Yucatán
Cancún
Gulf of Mexico

Gulf of Honduras
Belmopan
BELIZE
GUATEMALA
San Pedro Sula
HONDURAS
Guatemala City
San Salvador
EL SALVADOR
Tegucigalpa
NICARAGUA
Managua
Lake Nicaragua
COSTA RICA
San José
PANAMA
Panama City
Gulf of Panama

Barranquilla
Cartagena
Golfo del Darién
Gulf of Venezuela
Sincelejo
Montería
Medellín
Bucaramanga
Cúcuta
San Cristóbal
Lake Maracaibo
Mérida
Bogotá
Villavicencio
COLOMBIA
Cali
Buenaventura
Manizales
Armenia
Pereira
Ibagué
Cordillera Central
Cordillera Occidental
Cordillera Oriental
Meta
Guaviare
Florencia
Pasto
Caquetá
Putumayo
Orinoco
Negro
Pico da Neblina 3014

ECUADOR
Quito
Volcán Cotopaxi 5896
Chimborazo 6310
Guayaquil
Machala
Alausí
Iquitos
Amazon
Marañón
Napo

PERU
Lima
Trujillo
Chiclayo
Piura
Chimbote
Nevado de Huascarán 6768
Pucallpa
Ucayali
Ayacucho
Cusco
Cajamarca

BRAZIL
Selvas
Juruá
Javari
Juruá
Purus
Madeira
Rio Branco
Japurá

BOLIVIA

Equator

30°N 20°N 10°N 0° 10°S

130°W 120°W 110°W 100°W 90°W 80°W 70°W

VERMONT
MAINE
NEW HAMPSHIRE
MASSACHUSETTS
RHODE ISLAND
CONNECTICUT
NEW YORK
NEW JERSEY
PENNSYLVANIA
DELAWARE
MARYLAND
DISTRICT OF COLUMBIA
WEST VIRGINIA
VIRGINIA
Washington D.C.
NORTH CAROLINA
SOUTH CAROLINA
OHIO
MICHIGAN
INDIANA
KENTUCKY
TENNESSEE
GEORGIA
ALABAMA
MISSISSIPPI
FLORIDA
WISCONSIN
ILLINOIS
MINNESOTA
IOWA
MISSOURI
ARKANSAS
LOUISIANA
NORTH DAKOTA
SOUTH DAKOTA
NEBRASKA
KANSAS
OKLAHOMA
TEXAS
MONTANA
WYOMING
COLORADO
NEW MEXICO
IDAHO
UTAH
ARIZONA
WASHINGTON
OREGON
NEVADA
CALIFORNIA

ALASKA

HAWAII

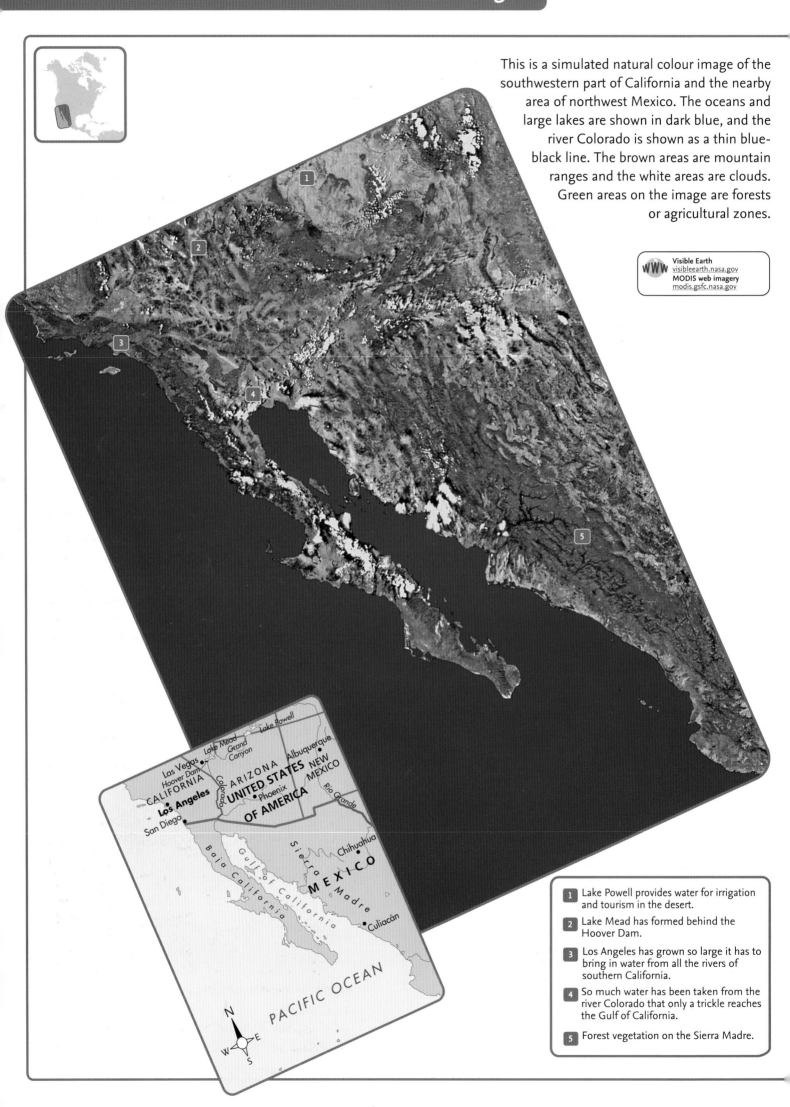

This is a simulated natural colour image of the southwestern part of California and the nearby area of northwest Mexico. The oceans and large lakes are shown in dark blue, and the river Colorado is shown as a thin blue-black line. The brown areas are mountain ranges and the white areas are clouds. Green areas on the image are forests or agricultural zones.

WWW **Visible Earth**
visibleearth.nasa.gov
MODIS web imagery
modis.gsfc.nasa.gov

1 Lake Powell provides water for irrigation and tourism in the desert.

2 Lake Mead has formed behind the Hoover Dam.

3 Los Angeles has grown so large it has to bring in water from all the rivers of southern California.

4 So much water has been taken from the river Colorado that only a trickle reaches the Gulf of California.

5 Forest vegetation on the Sierra Madre.

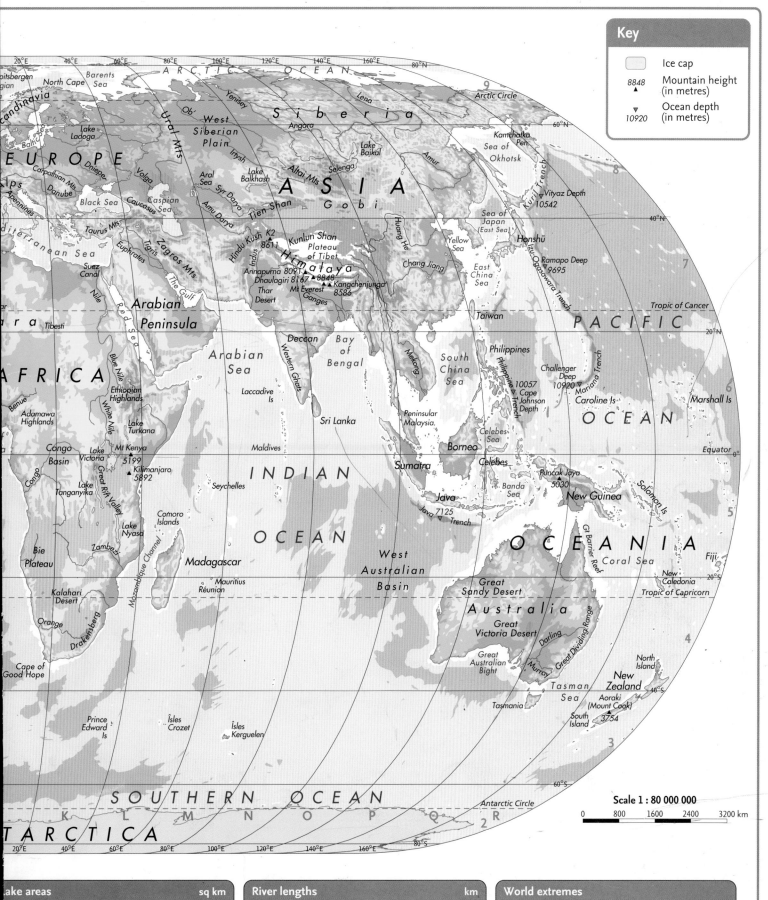

Key

☐	Ice cap
▲ 8848	Mountain height (in metres)
▼ 10920	Ocean depth (in metres)

Scale 1 : 80 000 000

0	800	1600	2400	3200 km

Lake areas	sq km
Caspian Sea	371 795
Lake Superior	82 100
Lake Victoria	68 800
Lake Huron	59 600
Lake Michigan	57 800
Lake Tanganyika	32 900
Great Bear Lake	31 328
Lake Baikal	30 500
Lake Nyasa	30 044

River lengths	km
Nile (Africa)	6695
Amazon (S. America)	6516
Chang Jiang (Asia)	6380
Mississippi-Missouri (N. America)	5969
Ob'-Irtysh (Asia)	5568
Yenisey-Angara-Selenga (Asia)	5500
Huang He (Asia)	5464
Congo (Africa)	4667
Río de la Plata-Paraná (S. America)	4500
Mekong (Asia)	4425

World extremes	
Highest mountain	
Mt Everest (Asia)	8848 m
Largest inland water area	
Caspian Sea	371 795 sq km
Largest island	
Greenland	2 175 600 sq km
Longest river	
Nile (Africa)	6695 km
Deepest water	
Mariana Trench (Pacific Ocean)	10 920 m

Eckert IV projection

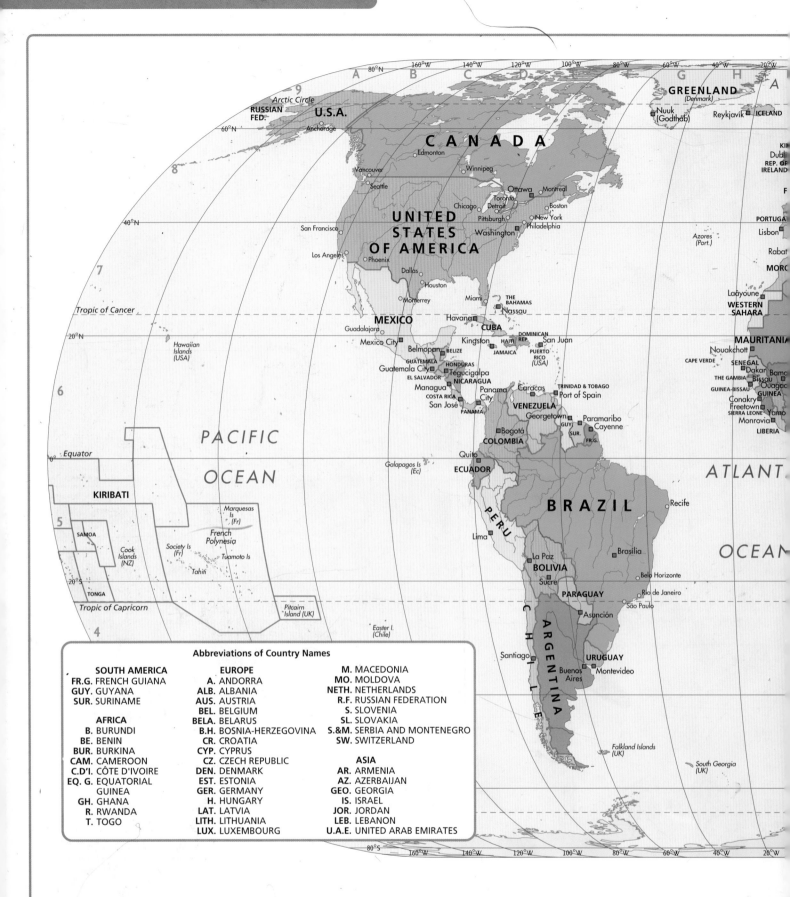

Abbreviations of Country Names

SOUTH AMERICA	EUROPE	M. MACEDONIA
FR.G. FRENCH GUIANA	A. ANDORRA	MO. MOLDOVA
GUY. GUYANA	ALB. ALBANIA	NETH. NETHERLANDS
SUR. SURINAME	AUS. AUSTRIA	R.F. RUSSIAN FEDERATION
	BEL. BELGIUM	S. SLOVENIA
AFRICA	BELA. BELARUS	SL. SLOVAKIA
B. BURUNDI	B.H. BOSNIA-HERZEGOVINA	S.&M. SERBIA AND MONTENEGRO
BE. BENIN	CR. CROATIA	SW. SWITZERLAND
BUR. BURKINA	CYP. CYPRUS	
CAM. CAMEROON	CZ. CZECH REPUBLIC	ASIA
C.D'I. CÔTE D'IVOIRE	DEN. DENMARK	AR. ARMENIA
EQ. G. EQUATORIAL	EST. ESTONIA	AZ. AZERBAIJAN
GUINEA	GER. GERMANY	GEO. GEORGIA
GH. GHANA	H. HUNGARY	IS. ISRAEL
R. RWANDA	LAT. LATVIA	JOR. JORDAN
T. TOGO	LITH. LITHUANIA	LEB. LEBANON
	LUX. LUXEMBOURG	U.A.E. UNITED ARAB EMIRATES

Time Comparisons

Time varies around the world due to the earth's rotation causing different parts of the world to be in light or darkness at an one time. To account for this, the world is divided into twenty-four Standard Time Zones based on 15° intervals of longitude

1:00am	2:00am	3:00am	4:00am	5:00am	6:00am	7:00am	8:00am	9:00am	10:00am	11:00am	no
Samoa Tonga (next day)	Hawaiian Is Cook Is Tahiti	Anchorage	Vancouver Seattle Los Angeles	Edmonton Phoenix	Winnipeg Chicago Mexico City	New York Miami Lima	Puerto Rico La Paz Asunción	Nuuk Brasília Buenos Aires	South Georgia	Azores Cape Verde	Reyk Lon Free

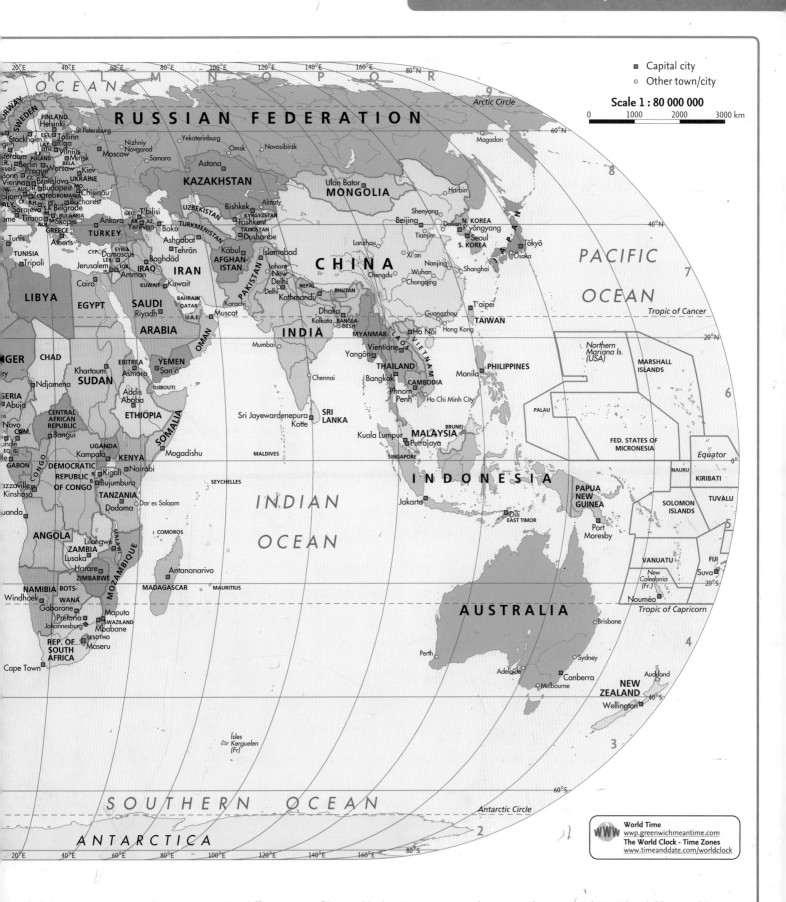

Capital city
○ **Other town/city**

Scale 1 : 80 000 000

0   1000   2000   3000 km

ARCTIC OCEAN

RUSSIAN FEDERATION

Arctic Circle

SWEDEN
FINLAND
Helsinki
St Petersburg
Nizhniy Novgorod
Yekaterinburg
Omsk
Novosibirsk
Magadan
Stockholm
Riga
Tallinn
Moscow
Samara
Astana
KAZAKHSTAN
Vilnius
Minsk
POLAND
Berlin
Warsaw
Kiev
UKRAINE
Bishkek
UZBEKISTAN
Ulan Bator
MONGOLIA
Harbin
Shenyang
Prague
Bratislava
Budapest
Chisinau
ROMANIA
Bucharest
T'bilisi
Almaty
KYRGYZSTAN
Tashkent
Beijing
N. KOREA
P'yongyang
Dalian
Zagreb
Belgrade
Ankara
Yerevan
Baku
TURKMENISTAN
TAJIKISTAN
Dushanbe
Lanzhou
Seoul
S. KOREA
Tokyo
Osaka
Tirana
Skopje
GREECE
Athens
TURKEY
Damascus
Ashgabat
Tehran
Kabul
AFGHAN-ISTAN
Islamabad
CHINA
Xi'an
Nanjing
Shanghai
PACIFIC OCEAN
TUNISIA
Tripoli
Jerusalem
Amman
IRAQ
Baghdad
IRAN
Lahore
New Delhi
PAKISTAN
Chengdu
Wuhan
Chongqing
Tropic of Cancer
Cairo
KUWAIT
Kuwait
BAHRAIN
QATAR
Delhi
NEPAL
Guangzhou
T'aipei
LIBYA
EGYPT
SAUDI
Riyadh
U.A.E.
Muscat
Kathmandu
BHUTAN
Dhaka
BANGLA-DESH
Hong Kong
TAIWAN
ARABIA
OMAN
INDIA
MYANMAR
Ha Noi
NIGER
CHAD
Khartoum
ERITREA
Asmara
YEMEN
San'a
Mumbai
Vientiane
LAOS
VIETNAM
THAILAND
Bangkok
PHILIPPINES
Manila
Northern Mariana Is. (USA)
MARSHALL ISLANDS
Ndjamena
SUDAN
Addis Ababa
DJIBOUTI
Chennai
CAMBODIA
Phnom Penh
Ho Chi Minh City
PALAU
Abuja
CENTRAL AFRICAN REPUBLIC
Bangui
ETHIOPIA
SOMALIA
Sri Jayewardenepura Kotte
SRI LANKA
BRUNEI
MALAYSIA
FED. STATES OF MICRONESIA
Equator
GABON
UGANDA
Kampala
KENYA
Mogadishu
MALDIVES
Kuala Lumpur
Putrajaya
SINGAPORE
NAURU
KIRIBATI
DEMOCRATIC REPUBLIC OF CONGO
Kinshasa
Kigali
Bujumbura
Nairobi
SEYCHELLES
INDONESIA
PAPUA NEW GUINEA
SOLOMON ISLANDS
TUVALU
TANZANIA
Dodoma
Dar es Salaam
INDIAN OCEAN
Jakarta
Dili
EAST TIMOR
Port Moresby
ANGOLA
ZAMBIA
Lusaka
Lilongwe
COMOROS
VANUATU
FIJI
Suva
Harare
ZIMBABWE
MOZAMBIQUE
Antananarivo
MADAGASCAR
MAURITIUS
New Caledonia (Fr.)
NAMIBIA
BOTS-WANA
AUSTRALIA
Tropic of Capricorn
Windhoek
Gaborone
Maputo
SWAZILAND
Mbabane
Brisbane
Noumea
Pretoria
Johannesburg
LESOTHO
Maseru
Perth
Sydney
Adelaide
Canberra
Auckland
REP. OF SOUTH AFRICA
Melbourne
NEW ZEALAND
Cape Town
Wellington

Isles Kerguelen (Fr)

SOUTHERN OCEAN

Antarctic Circle

ANTARCTICA

WWW World Time
wwp.greenwichmeantime.com
The World Clock - Time Zones
www.timeanddate.com/worldclock

The table below gives examples of times observed at different parts of the world when it is 12 noon in the zone at the Greenwich Meridian (0° longitude). The time at 0° is known as Greenwich Mean Time (GMT).

Crustal plates

The earth is made up of three main layers.

The outer layer, known as the crust, ranges in thickness from a few kilometres under the oceans to almost 50 km under mountain ranges.

The middle layer, known as the mantle, makes up 82% of the earth's volume. At the centre (core) of the earth, temperatures reach 4300 °C.

————	Plate boundary
←——→	Direction of movement

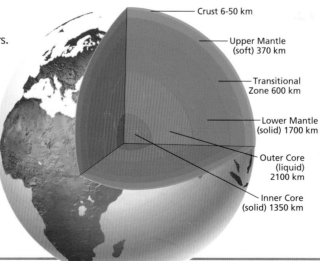

Crust 6-50 km

Upper Mantle (soft) 370 km

Transitional Zone 600 km

Lower Mantle (solid) 1700 km

Outer Core (liquid) 2100 km

Inner Core (solid) 1350 km

Earthquakes

Earthquakes occur most frequently along the junction of the plates which make up the earth's crust.

They are caused by the release of stress which builds up at the plate edges. When shock waves from these movements reach the surfac they are felt as earthquakes which may result in severe damage to property or loss of lives.

● High magnitude earthquake (over 7.8 on Richter scale)

See page 36 for explanation of Richter scale